Adolph Saphir

Our life-day

thoughts on John 9:4

Adolph Saphir

Our life-day

thoughts on John 9:4

ISBN/EAN: 9783741196096

Printed in Europe, USA, Canada, Australia, Japan

Cover: Foto ©Lupo / pixelio.de

More available books at **www.hansebooks.com**

OUR LIFE-DAY.

THOUGHTS ON JOHN IX. 4.

BY

REV. ADOLPH SAPHIR, D.D.,

AUTHOR OF
"LECTURES ON THE EPISTLE TO THE HEBREWS;"
"THE HIDDEN LIFE;" ETC.

NEW YORK:
ROBERT CARTER AND BROTHERS,
530, BROADWAY.

PREFACE.

THE following pages contain Addresses delivered this autumn on Sunday mornings to my congregation. They are published in compliance with the desire expressed by many of my hearers. With the exception of a few additional paragraphs, and a slight alteration of arrangement, they appear as they were spoken. May the Lord's blessing go with them.

A. S.

TRINITY PRESBYTERIAN CHURCH,
    NOTTING HILL,
        December, 1878.

CONTENTS.

CHAPTER I.
THE EARTHLY LIFE-DAY OF THE ETERNAL SON . . PAGE 1

CHAPTER II.
FIVE CHARACTERISTICS OF CHRIST'S LIFE . . . 32

CHAPTER III.
THE EXAMPLE OF CHRIST IN THE LIGHT AND LIFE OF THE SPIRIT 51

CHAPTER IV.
THE UNITY OF OUR LIFE, AND ITS RELATION TO ETERNITY 76

CHAPTER V.
FROM MORN TO EVE: THE SIX AGES OF MAN . . 107
    I. Infancy 118
    II. Childhood 122
    III. Youth 130
    IV. Manhood 140
    V. "Towards Evening" 155
    VI. Old Age 157

"I MUST WORK THE WORKS OF HIM THAT SENT ME, WHILE IT IS DAY: THE NIGHT COMETH, WHEN NO MAN CAN WORK."

John ix. 4

OUR LIFE-DAY.

CHAPTER I.

The Earthly Life-day of the Eternal Son.

"I must work the works of Him that sent Me, while it is day: the night cometh, when no man can work. As long as I am in the world, I am the Light of the world."—*John* ix. 4.

THE practical exhortation which is contained in these words is as obvious as it is solemn: "Whatsoever thy hand findeth to do, do it with thy might; for there is no work, nor device, nor knowledge, nor wisdom, in the grave, whither thou goest."* God, who has assigned to each of us his work, and who has entrusted to each gifts and opportunities, has also fixed the length of time during which the task has to be performed, and the stewardship to be

* Ecclesiastes ix. 10.

exercised. Within the limits ordained by Him the work must be done, or it remains for ever unaccomplished. The time for sowing the seed, for laying out our talent on usury, for laying up for ourselves treasure in heaven, is definite; the night cometh, and with it the termination of our labour.

All men have felt this, and have spoken of life as short when compared with the magnitude and difficulty of life-work.* This thought fills us with sadness and humility, while it exhorts to diligence and concentrated persevering energy. But it assumes a more solemn significance when we remember that the life-work is a task imposed by God, who is both the bountiful Giver and the righteous Judge. "Life is short," say the Jewish fathers, "the work is great, the Master is urgent."† The remembrance of God and the prospect of judgment invest the thought of our short life-day with solemnity, and lead conscience and heart to seek divine grace and help; and thus we find that Israel, viewing life in the light of divine revelation, humbled by the sin-convincing law, and comforted by the promise of redeeming mercy, finds its refuge in God, who is from everlasting to everlasting, the dwelling of His people in all generations. The prayer of Moses, the man of

* "Ars longa, vita brevis." † Pirke Aboth.

God, when he thinks of the short and fleeting character of life, is, "So teach us to number our days, that we may apply our hearts unto wisdom."* It is a necessary prayer for all who in the wilderness of time are journeying on to the land of eternity; for only divine grace can teach us this lesson, simple and obvious though it be. For the heart will not apply itself, give itself, discipline itself, unto wisdom, because, taken up, divided, and diverted from the one great centre by the multiform and ever-changing desires and pursuits of earthly and time-things, it forgets the one great and inevitable end to which we hasten —the appearing of our ultimate self, with its finished life-work, before God in eternity.

Such is the exhortation which, in the words of Christ, appeals with solemn and immediate conviction to our heart and conscience. But Jesus never merely repeats the teaching of human reason, observation, and conscience, or even the demands of the divine law. Every truth announced by Him receives in His words its deepest exposition, and its highest manifestation. He brings out its most profound meaning; He expands it to its utmost limits; He traces it to its deepest root. And He not merely as the perfect Prophet fully unfolds

* Psalm xc. 12.

all truth, but as the divine Mediator, the Redeemer, and the Example of His people, He fulfils in Himself all truths and precepts; thus revealing to us the only source from whence we can derive strength to follow Him, and to obey the word of God. Jesus reveals to us truth, and the only way of our living the truth, by unfolding to us His own inner life, by communicating to us His own experience, and by sending His Spirit into our hearts. All His words point to His priestly and royal office; for by His death, resurrection, and the sending of the Comforter, He gives Himself unto His people, and converts all His teaching into giving—His self-manifestation into communication of life and love.

The words which we are now considering express, as it were, the philosophy of Christ's life, the rule and method which regulated all His steps and works; but they also point out the source from which He derived constant and joyous strength in His path, the uninterrupted communion with the Father, out of which proceeded all His actions. We can follow Christ's example only in Christ's way; not merely the walk, but the method of the walk is set before us as our model. Hence by directing your attention to the inner life of our Lord, as His words reveal it in its deepest root, His union with the Father, I do not wish to divert you from the practical exhortation of His solemn utterance, but rather to point out the only sure foundation on which it is possible for us to build our imitation of His example.

Although this word of Christ may be considered as the motto and superscription of His whole life, yet the occasion on which it was uttered throws abundant light on its meaning. The Lord and His disciples were deeply impressed when they saw the man which had been born blind.* He seemed to them a type of human misery and suffering. Both in the minds of the disciples and of our Lord, thought and feeling were stirred by this sad spectacle. The question of the disciples contains elements of truth, which we are apt to overlook in our criticism of its error. Misery cannot be traced to God's creative goodness, wisdom, and power. The original purpose of Divine love was that human eyes, wonderfully formed to be light-receptive, should behold the light; that the sun, which God created and appointed to be a luminary by day, should bring gladness to man, and make his step sure and joyous. It was natural for the disciples, who knew the law of God,

* John ix. 1–3.

and had been under the teaching of Moses, to connect misery with sin, and to trace suffering to the transgression of God's precepts. Nor was it contrary to the revealed method of divine providence, or to experience, to imagine that the iniquity of the fathers was visited on the children even to the third and fourth generation.

But our Lord not merely corrects the error of the disciples, which reminds us of the false reasoning of Job's friends; His whole attitude to the problem of misery is different from theirs. While the disciples looked to the origin and cause of this suffering, our Lord looked forward to its removal and healing. They asked, "Who is to blame?" Jesus asked, "Who is to save?" The disciples wondered by whose guilt the beautiful work of God had been thus marred. Jesus saw in this man's blindness, in all human misery, only the occasion for the manifestation of the healing and restoring, the salvation-works of God. Instead of looking towards the dark abyss, out of which sin and misery originate, the Lord's heart looks to the glory of God, who by redemption exalts fallen man to even higher blessedness than that of creaturely innocence. And therefore Jesus feels Himself under the irresistible necessity, "I must work the works of Him that sent me." Jesus looks upon sin, misery, want, sorrow, death, only that He may bring pardon, healing, abundance, consolation, and life. He came not to judge and to condemn, but to save, to rescue; not to describe, analyse, and denounce the disease of sin, but to heal it; not to scrutinize and lament over the world's iniquity, but to be the Saviour of mankind, the Physician and Restorer, the Shepherd, seeking and saving the lost. The world has had no lack of philosophers and moralists who describe and tabulate with acutest analysis and subtle discrimination moral evil and the misery and suffering of mankind; there have always been poets who, with profound sensitiveness and with touching pathos, have given expression to all the various discords, sorrows, passions, griefs, and despairs which agitate human hearts and lives and nations; there have arisen many legislators and theorists who have endeavoured to cure or to alleviate the sad diseases of society by laws, institutions, and regulations. But the world has seen only one Jesus, "the Lamb of God, which taketh away the sin of the world;" only One, who came to rescue, to lay down His own life, that the world through Him might be saved.

Only one Jesus! but this one divine Lord has many representatives, many followers, in whom He lives, whom He energizes by His Spirit, and by whom He continues His work of saving, healing, and renewing power. The words of Jesus suggest to us our own task, and furnish us with the key-note of our life. It is the tendency and practice of the natural man to ask, "Whose fault is it?" whenever he sees disorder and suffering; it ought to be the tendency and practice of the Christian to ask, "Am I not sent to remedy, to heal, to comfort?" He is in the world as Jesus was in the world. When Jesus, in the synagogue of Nazareth, opened the book of the prophet Isaiah, He found the place where the mission of the Christ is described, and He said, "This day is this Scripture fulfilled in your ears." What was this mission? It was to bring to the poor the evangel of peace; to the broken-hearted, healing; to the captives, deliverance; to the blind the recovering of sight; and to the bruised, liberty. The Christian is sent forth by Christ. Jesus manifested His own forgiving love, His own all-conquering and heart-renewing power. The Christian manifests the love of Jesus, which has brought pardon and renewal to his own heart, and with which he now goes forth to love and to announce divine love to his fellow-man. He exerts the power of Christ, which has subdued his own sin, healed his own disease and restored his soul to fellowship with God and to strength of obedience; in the very power of Christ and by the indwelling of Christ's mind, he loves, helps, restores. While he is in the world, it is his desire to be the witness and the channel of redeeming grace and power.

Our Lord leads us however still deeper into the inner sanctuary of His life. He does not say, "I must save and heal; I must perform the works which are my delight;" although this would have been true. Jesus points out to us that in all His acts, in all words and works of His self-manifestion, He acts in communion with the Father, and in obedience to His will. He reveals to us the one source, from which flow both His labour and His joy—the infinitely sweet and tender, the uninterrupted communion between Him and the Father. Thus even in His childhood it was an inward necessity with Him to be in the spiritual, heavenly element; but the way in which He expresses this brings before us not so much His own spiritual mind and choice as His abiding near and in the Father. "Must I not be about the things of my Father?" It was His delight to speak to the poor sinful woman, who came to the well of Sychar, of the gift of God, the living water. But when He explains to the disciples why His soul had been so refreshed that He needed no food for the body, which had been weary and exhausted, He points again to the Father: "My meat is to do the will of Him that sent Me, and to finish His work." He, who manifested His own glory in every miracle which He performed, explains to His chosen disciples in the night when He spoke to them plainly: "The Father that dwelleth in Me, He doeth the works." He, who in all His words and teachings revealed Himself as the Saviour, the Fountain of Living Water, the Bread of Life, declares, "I have not spoken of myself; but the Father which sent Me, He gave Me a commandment, what I should say, and what I should speak." *

In no gospel is the divinity of our Lord so clearly and frequently brought before us as in the gospel of John; in no portion of Scripture is such constant emphasis laid on the communion between the Father and the Son, and on the subordination of the Son to the Father, in the counsel and work of redemption. This was the joy of Christ; not merely that He performed the great salvation works, but that He performed them by abiding in His Father's love, and by His Father dwelling in Him. This was His joy and reward,

* Luke ii. 49; John iv. 33, xiv. 10, 24, xii. 48-50.

that the Father loved Him, because He laid down His life for the sheep; that the Father was glorified and manifested in Him; that it was the Father's indwelling in Him which was the strength, the animating spirit, of all His works. And thus every word and act of Christ was not merely a manifestation of the Father to the world, but it was also a process of inward communion and growth, even as the Lord most simply describes it by saying, "I live *by* the Father," and, "This is my *meat*, to do the will of Him that sent me."

This perfect communion proceeds from the essential and eternal union between the Father and the Son. Here is the great mystery of godliness, *God* manifest in the flesh. The Lord, the Anointed, who came as the Sent One, and was obedient unto death, even the death of the cross, said from all eternity, "Lo, I come to do thy will." Could Jesus have declared the Father, whom no man hath seen at any time, unless He was "the only-begotten Son, which is in the bosom of the Father"?* Could He be the mediator and channel of divine love, unless He could say, "Thou lovedst Me before the foundation of the world"?† How could He give unto His sheep eternal life, and keep them in perfect and everlasting safety, unless He and the

Father are one?* And what is our hope, but that He will bring us unto glory, and present us to His Father, "Behold I and the children whom Thou hast given Me"?† To believe that Jesus is the Son of God is the Christian's blessedness and strength.

If we have thus by the words of our Lord been brought to behold His communion with the Father, rooted in His eternal union with Him, as the source and strength of His life, we have arrived at that point which apparently abstract, doctrinal and mysterious, contains the most practical and comprehensive principle of the Christian life. Apart from Christ we can do nothing; abiding in Him we bring forth fruit, and glorify the Father. The great question therefore is, What is meant by abiding in Christ? The Lord explains to us both the nature and the method of this communion. "As the Father hath loved Me, so have I loved you: continue ye in my love. If ye keep my commandments, ye shall abide in my love; even as I have kept my Father's commandments, and abide in His love."‡ We stand then in the same relation to Jesus as the Lord stands to His heavenly Father. Jesus sent by the

---

* John x. 27-30. † Heb. ii. 13.
‡ John xv. 9, 10.

Father; we sent by the Lord Jesus. Jesus by an inward necessity working the works of Him that sent Him; we by the power of the Spirit, whom we have received through the glorified humanity of our Lord, constrained and strengthened to continue the works of Christ, to deliver His message, to manifest His love, to exert His power. Jesus abiding in the Father's love, enjoying communion with Him, growing in strength, and sustaining and renewing His spiritual life in His very activity and self-manifestation to the world; we in like manner abiding in Christ, growing more deeply and firmly rooted in Him, and receiving Christ's joy, so as to make our joy full, by our doing the things which Christ commanded us. Christ manifesting the Father; we manifesting Christ. Jesus the light of the world; we also the light of the world by virtue of Christ dwelling in us. But the sure foundation on which this wonderful union and identity between Christ and us rests is none other than this: Jesus is the only-begotten of the Father. As the Father hath life in Himself, so hath He given the Son to have life in Himself. The eternal union between Father, Son and Spirit, and the union of the divine and human natures in the one person of our adorable Saviour Jesus Christ, form the essential and immovable foundation of the mystical yet most real union between Christ and the Church. And thus in our daily experience, and for our earthly path, with its duties and trials, we have an eternal and inexhaustible fountain of love and light. It is because Jesus is the true vine, and His Father the husbandman, that we, who were once dead in trespasses and sins, are now branches which bring forth fruit; that we are the body, of which Christ is the Head to the glory of the Father.

The tendency of the present day is to lay stress on what is regarded as "practical;" that is, what is thought to exert an immediate and powerful influence on man's character and conduct. The doctrine of Scripture, the revelation of God and of His counsel—theology in short—is considered as something abstruse and theoretical; the great and important topic, it is held, is the development of human character, and the true fulfilment of duty in the various relationships of life. The root of this tendency lies very deep, and its spirit is diametrically opposed to that of Scripture—of Jehovahism in the Old, and Christianity in the New Testament. Scripture is "practical." Its aim is, that the man of God should be furnished unto every good work; that we should be wise unto salvation, and glorify God both now and for evermore. But as Scripture regards man's departure from God as the essence of all sin and misery, it declares that in God alone is our remedy and salvation. To know God and Jesus Christ is life eternal. To be brought into communion with the only fountain of life, light, and love, is the only redemption for man. "I am the Lord thy God," is the sum and substance of the Old Testament teaching; and as this is the fundamental truth, so it is all-sufficient. It is the foundation on which all commandments rest; it is the only source from which men can derive strength to obey divine precepts; it is the only consolation and hope for sinful and heavy-laden humanity. And in the New Testament God is perfectly revealed. The name of Father, Son, and Holy Ghost, into which we are baptized, is to us Christians not an abstruse and speculative dogma, but the very element of light and love in which we live, the source from which we derive all strength and consolation for our earthly life. The Father's love to the Son, eternal, infinite, and unchangeable, is our ultimate stay and rest. It is to this inexhaustible treasury that we must retreat in the consciousness of our sin and unworthiness. If we only knew the love which God has to the world, to that which is finite and created, fallen and sinful, we would not know a love which is boundless—we would not know that God *is* love. God's love in creation, and God's love in redemption, have indeed the same source. But God's love in creation is limited. It is dependent on the obedience of the creature; it may be obscured, nay it may be changed into wrath, by the sin of man or angel. But the love of redemption is one with the infinite and unchanging love of the Father to the Son. It is out of God's infinite love within Himself, the love of the Father to the Son, that His redeeming love to the world flowed. It is for this reason that God revealed *Himself*, His own eternal love, when He sent Jesus into the world. The promise of eternal life was given to us in Christ Jesus before the world began; and we who believe are loved by the Father as He loved the Son; and it is this divine love which is now in us. The life which the Christian possesses, and the love which is shed abroad in his heart by the Holy Ghost, are in the strict sense of the word divine; and this renders the writings of the apostle John so profoundly practical to believers, that he shows unto us in the mystery of the Trinity the perfect objective character of life and love which through faith become ours.*

* 1 Tim. ii. 1; Titus i. 2; 1 John, *passim*.

Learn also that all things pertaining to life and salvation are freely given to us, and that the grace whereby we are to walk in Christ's footsteps is treasured up in Christ's fulness. It is not by obeying Christ's commandments that we can *enter* into His love. We cannot merit it, or make ourselves worthy of it. It is the free and unspeakable gift of grace. "As the Father hath loved Me, so have I loved you." Jesus was the infinite, perfect, and adequate object of the Father's love from all eternity. Jesus, as undertaking in the eternal covenant our redemption, was the Father's Beloved, and all things were given into His hand. Jesus, the Incarnate Son, glorified the Father by His holy and constant obedience, and the manifestation of perfect service in the filial spirit drew forth continually the Father's delight. The love of the Father to the Son, as Messiah, most touchingly described in the prophet Isaiah, is still more clearly brought before us in the gospel. The voice from the excellent glory is heard: "This is my beloved Son, in whom I am well pleased." It is because the disciples, the men whom the Father hath chosen out of the world, and for whom Christ laid down His life, are beheld by the Father in Christ, that this eternal and infinite love includes also all poor and lost sinners. As the Father hath loved

Christ, with this very love and in this very love the Saviour loves us. The Father and the Son are eternally and essentially one. Their oneness is revealed to us in this, that the Father knew the Son, and the Son knew the Father, *in the counsel of redemption*, viz., that the Son should lay down His life for the sheep. It is therefore the Father's love to the Son which is the source, strength, and reward of the Son's love to us.*

We must receive this wonderful love of Christ by faith. It is heaven-high above us, it descends as a royal gift. Apart from works, and notwithstanding all our sins, it is bestowed upon us. Before our birth, even before the foundation of the world, it was ours in the mind and heart of our Redeemer-God. If we understand what is implied in God's salvation—viz., our adoption, and our being glorified together with Christ—we must see at once that its origin can only be in the purpose which the Father purposed in Himself, and that our experience of divine grace is "according as He hath chosen us in Christ before the foundation of the world." Law and gospel are contrasted as creaturely and divine, temporal and eternal, cosmical and heavenly; in Christ Jesus

---

* John x. 15, 17; xvii.

divine righteousness, love, and glory are revealed and given unto all who believe.

But if we wish to *abide* in this love, Christ teaches us that we must keep His commandments. And yet He has no other commandment but to abide in Him, to lean on His strength, to live by His word, to rely on His promise, to look unto His example, to fix our heart on Him. Then our life will be a manifestation of Christ's love and Spirit; we will show forth His praise, reflect His image, and walk in His ways. As the Son was free and full of joy in His obedience, as the Son had perfect rest in God while He laboured and toiled, as He continually received strength from the love and indwelling of the Father, so will Christ's love be an abiding joy to us in our obedience and suffering; it will be Christ's yoke and Christ's burden, and therefore easy and light. True, we are to serve, and Christ's disciples are taught to do whatsoever He commanded; but as Jesus says of the commandment He had received of the Father, "I know that His commandment is life everlasting;" so the believer whom Jesus sends into the world knows that the grace of Jesus gives and fulfils all His precepts, that of Him is our fruit found.*

* Phil. ii. 13; Hosea xiv. 8.

There is another feature in this saying of Christ which claims our attention, as it seems almost unparalleled in the gospel narrative. Perhaps no other words bring before us the life of our Lord in an aspect so human. Nowhere does He present His life on earth so completely on a level with ours, speaking of it, as we speak of ours, as a short, limited period, as a day, hastening on to the inevitable termination, the night. He views Himself here, as it were, *as a human day labourer.* In everything, sin excepted, He became like unto His brethren; and of the man Christ Jesus it may be said, according to the Lord's own expression, " Man goeth forth unto his work and to his labour until the evening."*

It is not without difficulty that we enter into this view. We know that Jesus was born in the fulness of time, and that then the dayspring from on high visited the world through the tender mercy of our God; but we never think of this commencement of His earthly history, without remembering that He came forth from the Father, and that He is the true and eternal Light, uncreated and before the world began. We know that He died upon the cross, and that after He had cried with a loud voice, He gave up the ghost. But we

* Psalm civ. 23.

never think or speak of His death without adding triumphantly, "Yea rather, that is risen again. He was dead; behold, He is alive for evermore." It is to the suffering Lord, whose life is offered for sin, that the promise was made and fulfilled, "He shall see His seed, He shall prolong His days, and the pleasure of the Lord shall prosper in His hand. Who can declare His generation?" Death is so little the termination of His work, that it may rather be viewed as the culminating-point of His life and obedience, and the starting-point of His high priestly and royal activity. His love and His work continued even amidst the bitter sufferings of His cross. He prayed for His enemies, He opened the kingdom of heaven to the sinner who turned to Him in faith, He remembered the loneliness of His mother and commended her to His loved disciple. His death was itself the greatest work ever accomplished, the greatest work which He Himself ever accomplished; it was *the* obedience by which everlasting righteousness was brought in, by which death was swallowed up in victory, Satan conquered, and life eternal secured to all the children of the New Covenant. Christ's death was the most perfect and glorious revelation of God, of His character and of His everlasting and hidden counsel. The work of Jesus as the prophet, the revealer of God, received its highest and deepest fulfilment on the cross. Here it is that the Only-begotten of the Father declares the name of God perfectly, reveals most fully the glory of God, and manifests depths of divine love and mercy, holiness and truth, which even angels had not known before.*

The Lord always looked forward to His death as His great work; He regarded it not as the end, but the beginning, as well as the true source of His true and never-ending influence and reign. While other men look upon death as the limit and termination of their work, Jesus from the very commencement of His ministry looks forward to the cross as the goal; and while continually directing His disciples to this great event, longs for the accomplishment of His baptism, and announces that from this mysterious elevation He will draw all men unto Himself.†

And after His death on the cross, and the rest of His body in the grave, when He had spoiled and triumphed over principalities and powers, the resurrection morn was the beginning of His glorious and unceasing activity. Since that day He has constantly appeared unto His

* Isaiah liii.; John xvii. 1.
† John xii. 32; ii. 18-21.

disciples, influenced them by His Spirit, nay, done greater works by them than He performed on earth. Without intermission He has interceded on behalf of His Church, while according to His promise He has been with His people all the days of the age, present in their assemblies, in their homes, and in their hearts, guiding, sustaining, teaching, and strengthening them in all their duties, trials, and sorrows. Nor is this all His work; for the government of the whole world is on His shoulders, and unto the incarnate Son of God, the Lamb that was slain, is given all power and rule in heaven and on earth.

When we think of this, we feel all the more both the condescending grace and the special purpose of the Lord's words: "I must work the works of Him that sent me, while it is day: the night cometh, when no man can work. As long as I am in the world, I am the Light of the world." Jesus presents Himself here as our example. He speaks of His life as a mission, a task, which had to be fulfilled within the limits of the time assigned by the Father. He thus assures us of His perfect sympathy with us in the view which we must take of our life-work, and of our short time for fulfilling it, while He lays open to our eyes the inmost motive-power of His own life, the secret of His sustained and perfect obedience, the wonderful combination of the filial and joyous Spirit with that of service and absolute obedience.

Our view is more specially concentrated on the years of His ministry. How short is this period; a little while only the Light was in the world; the Bridegroom with the disciples. Yet how inexhaustible is the life of these three years. Who can measure the depth and breadth and length and height of the words and works which this short space of time comprised?

From the day that after His baptism and victory in the wilderness He went forth into Galilee, teaching in their synagogues, and preaching the gospel of the kingdom, healing all manner of sicknesses and diseases, until that night when He said to the Father in the presence of His disciples, "And now I am no more in the world, and I come to Thee," how marvellous was His life and testimony. Think of His ministry in Galilee and Judea; of His manifestations of grace and consolation to the poor and needy; of His training of the apostles, the chosen messengers appointed to teach the whole world. Think of that brief life, which was the perfect, the ultimate revelation of the Father, the all-sided presentation of the divine law, the embodiment of all true obedience.

Throughout all centuries the Church of God will behold in Jesus, as He lived on earth, the countenance of the Father, the glory of the Only-begotten. His words and acts, nay, every feature recorded in the gospel narrative, will prove full of heavenly instruction, infallible guidance, and abiding consolation. Here we have what is divine and absolutely perfect brought out, revealed, and embodied in all that is sinlessly human. Three years unveil to us that which is highest and deepest, and this in all the extension and ramifications of our human life and relationships. Of this inexhaustible life Jesus gives us the inner principle, and in such condescending humility that we may be encouraged by His perfect sympathy, and learn of Him the method of divine love in our short life-day. He speaks to us as our fellow-pilgrim. He enters into the feeling which regards the fragrant morning of our childhood, and the bright, vigorous hours of our youth, and the full, matured work of our manhood, as passing away quickly, and which looks forward to evening and the setting sun as the end of all our earthly labour. Jesus also says, "The night cometh, when no man can work. As long as I am in the world, I am the Light of the world."

The night cometh. It is an absolute certainty. The night cometh as the termination of our earthly life-day and work. It is true that to the believer the night will bring peaceful rest. He falls asleep in Jesus. He enters into a state which is "far better." But it is true of the Christian, as well as of all men, that with the day's close all labour is at an end; and that as death finds us and our task, so we remain. When we appear before the judgment-seat of Christ we shall receive the things done *in our body*. Our reward will be for testimony, suffering, and service here on earth. The seedtime is over when we are called away from this life. It imparts to our present life an unspeakable solemnity; it endows it with an infinite preciousness and value. And while at first sight we may feel overpowered by the thought of the short space given to us for our labour, and inclined to feverish haste and to impatient self-made work, a truer insight will teach us that as the approach of the night is altogether beyond our calculation and control, so it behoves us, with calmest faith and implicit surrender of our own will, to look upon each day's work and each day's trial, as portioned out to us by divine wisdom and love. How much of false zeal, self-chosen work, and self-appointed times, is there in our own private and in our public Christian life. We run before we are sent; we choose the kind of usefulness and work for which we fancy we have inclination and adaptation; we select the times and method of accomplishing our task. We pursue with spurious zeal and self-sustained energy aims of our own choice; we hurry impatiently our own souls and those of others, and are satisfied with forced results, till experience teaches us, to our deep humiliation, that grace also has its nature and law, and that in God's work "it is not of him that willeth, nor of him that runneth, but of God that showeth mercy."

There is another and more excellent way. We are "created in Christ Jesus unto good works, which God hath before ordained that we should walk in them." We have not to make our path; the eternal wisdom of God has appointed it for us. We have not to seek it, but it runs past our very door; the fatherly providence and guidance of our Lord brings it close to us day by day. It is God's way, and not our own; we have only to follow Jesus, and to bring our will into subjection to the will of God. This method requires humility, and a constant surrender of our reason and will. It is easier to select a difficult task, and say to the Lord, "I would like to do this," than to ask, "What wilt Thou have me to do?" It is trying to our pride, and to what we imagine our highest and best feelings, when the day which we have hoped to devote to some labour is in God's providence filled with duties or sufferings which prevent our purposed activity. But it is the only true method of life which secures real and abundant work, and the peaceful consciousness that we are pleasing our Master, that we are relying on His help and blessing, and that we can cast the burden of our weakness, our fears, our errors, and our sins upon our loving and all-merciful Saviour.*

God can never mislead us. Though this be our last day on earth, we can make no better use of it than by fulfilling this day's task, by enduring patiently this day's trials, by showing a Christlike, loving spirit to our household, and to all with whom this day we are brought into contact. It is in this that the example of Jesus instructs us. Our Lord had no artificial and complicated path of life. Although He knew His time on earth would be short, He was in no feverish haste; but in calmness and with a steady rhythm He went through His work, and to His retreats of quiet and prayer. Day by day He was guided by His heavenly Father. He listened to the Father's voice. It woke Him early in the morning, and on Him He waited all the day. His soul was con-

* Eph. ii. 10; John xxii. 22; Acts ix. 6.

tinually filled with a holy fire, a burning zeal to fulfil His ministry, to do the will of the Father that sent Him. But so entirely were all His footsteps guided by the Father, and so exclusively was His desire to glorify the Father and to finish His work, that His life was calm and even; that all His words and works, and all the pauses in His work, were in accordance with the leadings of Providence, and hence no outward observer could see the constant strain and concentrated energy of His soul. He could not be hurried into any action by human calculation and the counsel of worldly wisdom. When His brethren advised Him to go up to the feast, the Lord pointed out, as one feature of the worldly mind, "Your time is alway ready." For they who do their own work and seek their own glory are also the masters and disposers of their time. But Jesus had "His time," and He knew when it was come. It was the Father's voice to which He responded, "Father, the hour is come." Our Lord did every thing in the right hour. He filled full every day given to Him. He did only one thing, and in that one thing all things—He abode in the Father's love.*

If we follow Jesus, we also shall be summoned

* Isa. l. 5; Ps. xxv. 5; Luke xii. 49, 50; John vii. 3-8; xii. 23; xvii. 1.

hence only when our work is accomplished. "The night cometh" to the faithful disciple when the heavenly all-wise and all-merciful Master considers the work done, and the race run. Let this assurance keep us in quiet and peaceful humility. Let not imagination dishonour the wisdom of God by fancying other circumstances and spheres of labour in which we could be more useful. Let not self-will question the perfect will of God, and the excellence of the mission on which He has sent us. Let us not be burdened with anxious care. Let us not be fettered by time-limited, unworthy aims. Let not the doubtful to-morrow, but the sure and blessed eternity, give hope to your heart, and strength and steadiness to your steps. Rejoice in to-day, God's loving gift, and look upon it as the time to work, to obey, to suffer, to grow in grace, and to praise the Lord in the land of this our earthly pilgrimage. Beyond the night is the bright morning of an everlasting harvest of perfect rest, of unmingled thanksgiving and adoration. In this prospect every day may be full of life and of work pleasing to God, and an everlasting possession. But no day without Christ. It is not night when He is near; and it is not day when He is absent. And without Christ means simply apart from Christ. Let not even good words and good works please us, unless they be uttered, unless they be done, *by Christ dwelling in us.* "My Father doth all things in Me," saith Christ. This was Christ's comfort, and to feel Christ do all in the soul is the comfort of every one that truly believeth on Him.

CHAPTER II.

Five Characteristics of Christ's Life.

"I must work the works of Him that sent Me, while it is day: the night cometh, when no man can work. As long as I am in the world, I am the Light of the world."—*John* ix. 4.

N these words of our Lord we find the expression of several peculiarities which characterised His life on earth.

1. The life of our Lord Jesus was the only complete human life which ever appeared. Our lives are but fragments; the life of Jesus was a perfect and glorious whole. He is the only One who could say with absolute truth, at the end of His earthly course, His life-day, "I have finished the work which thou gavest Me to do." He was the only One who had perfectly fulfilled the divine task assigned to Him, leaving nothing undone or incomplete; who had also done nothing, except what was included in that work, and in harmony with its spirit and scope. He was the

perfect servant of God, who, looking back on His day of service, knew that He had done the will of God—that will only, and that will completely. The universe never heard from human lips the words, "It is finished," as Jesus uttered them before He gave up the ghost and died.*

Jesus is the only One who truly lived the human life from beginning to end. All other lives and life-works are rather attempts than achievements. By reason of our constant errors and sins, of our weakness and impurity, our attempt is full of failure. We have frequently to retrace our steps, to undo as far as possible our work, to endure with bitter though vain regret the evil consequences and effects of the irreparable past. But in the walk of Jesus there was no hesitation, no faltering, no pause; He never stumbled, He never mistook the path, He never lost time by neglecting the opportunity, He never lost strength by not recognising the right and God-appointed hour. He was like the sun, "whose going forth is from the end of the heaven, and his circuit unto the ends of it." The path of this just Man was like the shining light, which shineth more and more unto the perfect day. All His steps were light and love. He filled full the

* John xvii. 4; xix. 30.

measure of life and life-work which the Father had given to Him. He walked in the good works which God had before ordained for Him with the joyous alacrity of the bridegroom coming out of his chamber, and the eager and vigorous energy of a strong man who runs a race. With perfect calmness, and with absolute peaceful certainty, He went on from strength to strength. In Him we behold the blessed Man of whom it is written, "He shall be like a tree ... that bringeth forth his fruit in his season; his leaf also shall not wither; and whatsoever he doeth shall prosper."*

The reason why the life of Jesus was perfect and complete was because His heart was *united* to glorify His Father. He was not like us, two-souled, double-minded; in Him there was only one centre and fountain—divine love. Hence the issues of life were pure and living streams, clear, full, and strong, gladdening and fertilizing the fields through which they ran their course. It was the singleness of His aim that rendered His life so full, so manifold, so united. It was the perfect heart that produced the perfect and complete life.†

* Psalm xix. 4–6; Prov. iv. 18; Psalm i. 3.
† διψυχοις, James i. 8; Prov. iv. 23.

The apostle Paul was perhaps more truly the follower of the Lord Jesus than any other disciple. He says unto us, "Be ye followers of me, even as I am of the Lord." Though we have only one Master, and only one absolute and perfect model, even Christ, yet divine grace, in condescension to our human weakness and our craving for human fellowship, may have appointed the life of the apostle Paul to be a special pattern to Christians, as we know his conversion is mercifully intended to be a pattern of divine grace and power, for the instruction and encouragement of all sinners. After Jesus appeared to him, and revealed Himself to his heart, the apostle seems never to have looked back, but to have pressed on, with intense concentration of purpose and marvellous singleness of heart, toward the mark of the "high calling of God in Christ Jesus." It was because he could say, "One thing I do," that his life was so rich and steadfast, his labours so abundant, his testimony so faithful, continuous, and many-sided. Hence when the time of his departure was at hand he was able to say, "I have finished my course." Yet how different is the disciple from the Master! For Paul had been once imperious, and only the grace of the Lord, which was abundant, and brought him life and faith, transplanted him into the kingdom of God. Paul had constantly to fight, to crucify the old man, and to experience that though he was spiritually-minded, there was another law in his members. When Paul exclaimed, "I have finished my course," he added no doubt inwardly, "Yet not I; it is by grace, it is Christ in me." Jesus is the only Perfect One; and from His earliest childhood day was linked to day by filial love and obedience to the Father.*

2. In the life of Jesus we see the perfect liberty of the Son in obedience and service. Here we behold the perfect unity of liberty and necessity. "I must" seems to us a hard word while we regard liberty our dearest and sweetest possession. It is because we do not fully understand what is meant by love that we find it difficult to see liberty and necessity in their essential and inseparable connection. But unto Jesus "I must" was identical with "It is my delight." He knew not the bondage of choice arising from a doubtful mind and a divided heart, from a will separate from the will of God, and at variance with His law. God's law was written on His heart; it was hidden there as His most precious, inviolable, and cherished treasure. As a child He said—wonderful expression in the mouth of a child; but there was no foolishness,

* Phil. iii. 13, 14; 2 Tim. iv. 6-8.

no waywardness, no opposition of self-asserting choice in that young heart—"I must be about my Father's business." "I must do the works of Him that sent Me" was the language of the Prophet of Galilee during His whole ministry. He showed His disciples that He *must* go unto Jerusalem, and suffer many things, and be crucified. He looked forward to His cross and death as the things that must be, that the Scripture be fulfilled. But this will to which He bowed was the Father's will; the necessity which He felt was rooted in the communion of life and love, which subsisted between the Father and the Son, and which was His joy and His strength. To obey the Father, and that by the Father's indwelling in Him, was the nourishment of Christ's life; it was His very delight.*

Here also is our true liberty, "I must work the works of Him that sent Me." We once experienced the bondage of another necessity when we were sold under sin; when the world was an irresistible magnet, and yet known to be an alien and hostile power; when our will was enslaved, and therefore a self-will.

As Martin Luther quaintly puts it: "Thou wilt say, But has not God given us a free-will? To

* Luke ii. 49; xxii. 37; Matt. xxv. 54.

which I answer, Why then wilt thou make it a self-will, and not allow it to remain free? If thou doest with thy will what pleases thee, it is no longer free, but thy own. God has not given to any one a self-will; this comes from Satan and Adam's fall. They turned their free-will, which they received from God, into a will of their own. For this is a free-will which wills nothing of its own, but looks only to God's will, whereby it remains free, and is caught and fettered by nothing. Thus it is in heaven, and we pray that it may be thus on earth."

We deceived ourselves for a time when, resisting the power of sin in our own strength, we fancied it was of him that willeth and runneth. But after the grace of God renewed our hearts and set free our will by the constraining power of Christ's love, we began to understand that the service of God is perfect freedom. Where the Spirit of the Lord is there is liberty. God works in us both to will and to do of His good pleasure. The new man delights in the law of God. Though sin still dwells in us, yet are we not in the flesh, but in the spirit; for the Spirit of God dwelleth in us. It is said of the Christian, in this his aspect of his spiritual regenerate condition: "Whosoever is born of God doth not commit sin; for his seed remaineth in him: and he cannot sin, because he is born of God."* But we have still the conflict with sin. We have still the daily task of crucifying the old man, of mortifying the members which are on earth. There is still within us the bondage of our self-will; and our constant struggle is to stand fast in the liberty with which Christ has made us free. In heaven we shall have fully attained the adoption, and possess the glorious liberty of the children of God. There sin will be an impossibility, holiness a necessity; for in perfect love liberty and necessity are united. Conformed to the image of God's own Son, we shall then be the children of God, serving God with body, soul, and spirit, no foreign element marring our nature and striving against our will.†

How strong and invincible, how calm and rich, is Jesus in this simple consciousness: "I must work the works of Him that sent me, while it is day." He is poor, yet He is free from care and irradiated with brightest serenity. He is surrounded by enemies and has no human protection, but He feels perfectly safe; and while His disciples remember that the Jews sought to kill Him, the Lord is only guided by the Spirit, by the

* Jer. xxxi. 33; 1 John iii. 9.
† Phil. iii. 21; 1 John iii. 2; Rom. viii. 29, 30.

desire to fulfil the Father's work.* He is Lord of all. In royal dignity and liberty, He who had not where to lay His head, dwelt on earth—the Son of God, the Son of man, the rightful heir.† In the service of God all things were His. He must work the works of the Father, and who can hinder or stay Him? No human power or sin; not even the gates of hell. "Behold, I cast out devils, and I do cures to-day and to-morrow, and the third day I shall be perfected."‡

If we follow Jesus we shall experience that "I must," instead of being a chain which fetters us, is a royal crown on our head; that seeking first God's kingdom and His righteousness, all other things are added to us; that He who sends us forth is our defence, though we be as sheep among wolves; that in all our weakness we are strong, and can overcome all difficulties, and in all our poverty we can make many rich.

3. Notice the wonderful union in Jesus of love to God and love to man. There is only one Love. Love to God and love to man are united in their origin and their nature. They form one river flowing out of the eternal love of God. If we truly love God, we love man. We cannot love

---

* John xi. 8–10. † Compare Matt. xvii. 24–27.
‡ Luke xiii. 32.

man aright unless we first love the Father. We find it difficult to combine harmoniously the two aspects of love. In our love to God there is so great an admixture of selfishness, self-will and self-seeking. In our love to man there is so much that is not spiritual, heavenly or eternal. Some of us find it easier to ascend to God with the wings of adoration and joyous contemplation, than to descend on the self-same ladder to our neighbour in the spirit, and with the service, of forgiving, comforting, and helping love. But in Jesus there was only one, deep, pure, divine love. When He healed the sick and opened the eyes of the blind, when He fed the multitude, when He cast out devils, when He taught the disciples, and blessed the little children, He was doing the works the Father had given Him to do, He beheld the countenance of the Father, and enjoyed communion with Him. When He prayed, and when He was alone with God, He felt the wants, the dangers, the sorrows of all His people, and His love continually rested on them. He was never alone, for the Father was always with Him; He was always alone, for He did all things heartily as unto the Father; He always dwelt in the secret place of the Most High, and all He said and did was an abiding in the Father's love.*

* John iii. 13; viii. 16; xvi. 32; Luke xxii. 32.

Hence that marvellous peculiarity of Jesus, that He stood alone, isolated from all men, not understood by any one, even as He was perfectly unfettered by human opinion, counsel, and expectations. He waited *only* upon God. He was from above. This we can see in all His life; and therefore was He the *Light* of the world, the Only-begotten of the Father, who is in the bosom of the Father. But He is also the Son of man, He loved man as Himself; and therefore was He the Light of the *world*.

Jesus Himself is the most luminous commentary on His own most beautiful saying concerning the two great commandments. Love to God comes first; love to man comes second, and yet is equal to the first. If we are in loving communion with Christ, our very dependence on Him, and loyalty to Him, as our one Master, will give us true liberty and inward independence from men and the world. Jesus came to minister; but He was Lord of all. And in like manner the Christian is, as Luther says, lord of all things by faith, and a servant of all in love. As we become strong in love, and learn to serve the brethren, and to regard our life as a life of ministry to Christ's disciples, as we become less selfish, so we become also less dependent on man, and look more exclusively to

Christ for guidance, approbation, encouragement, and reward. Our love to God becomes more intense, and yet the circle of our love to men enlarges. We live more alone and in secret with God, and yet we are more willing to spend and be spent for others.

We learn also from Jesus the essential connection between prayer and work; between our inner meditation and our outward activity. "I must *work*," says our Lord; the light cannot but shine. The true blessedness of the disciple is in hearing and doing the word.*

Christians must never forget that the predominant characteristic of their love on earth must be activity, the keeping His commandments. From time to time the Master calls us to rest awhile; we receive glimpses and foretastes of heavenly peace; but the purpose of God generally is, that by such exceptional seasons we may be strengthened to undertake new duties and new labours. Jesus descended from the Mount of Transfiguration, and met the sufferings and miseries of the world with healing power.

4. Jesus regarded His whole life as a *mission*. He spoke of Himself as one sent. He teaches on all occasions that He came to do the Father's will.

* Matt. vii. 24; John xiii. xvii. 4.

He views His whole life from this one point. It is His Father's will that Jesus should heal the broken-hearted, and declare glad tidings to the poor. It is His Father's will that Jesus should lay down His life for the sheep. It is the Father's will that whosoever believeth in the Son should have everlasting life, and that Jesus should raise him up at the last day.* There is a latent feeling in some as if the love and tenderness of Jesus were His in an exclusive sense, or at least in a higher degree than in the Father. We forget that when we behold Jesus forgiving the sinner, and receiving him with most tender compassion, when we behold Jesus permitting the woman to kiss His feet, we see the Father in Him—we see Him working the works which the Father gave Him to do. Jesus spoke and acted always as the Sent One, the Revelation and Representative of the Father; and it was this relationship continually realised, which was His strength and His joy. How bold and convincing is the expression of the apostle Paul: "God commendeth *His* love toward us, in that, while we were yet sinners, *Christ* died for us." We behold the Father's compassion in the tears of Jesus, and the Father's love in the blood of the Lamb. And thus when we approach God through Christ, we

* John x. 17, 18; vi. 39, 40.

appeal not merely to the work of Christ and to the love of Christ, we appeal not merely to Christ our righteousness, and to the grace of our Saviour, but we remind the Father of His own love which gave His Son; we appeal to the Father's love; we rest in the plea, "For Thy name's sake." Our ultimate foundation is, "I and the Father are one."

But as Jesus was *sent*, so it is likewise true that He *came*. It was His own free and sovereign will and good pleasure that He emptied Himself, that He became poor, that He took hold of the seed of Abraham, that He became Messiah, the Surety and Head of His people. His whole life on earth springs from the eternal love which in the covenant of grace moved the Son to the stupendous self-surrender which the apostle Paul describes in Phil. ii. 5–11. He came forth from the Father, even from of old, and from everlasting; and this voluntary coming of the Only-begotten invests His mission, His obedience unto death, with an infinite value and a transcendent glory. Here is our strong refuge, and our immovable rock: Jesus one with the Father; Jesus obedient to the Father. And here is the deepest meaning of Christ's example: "*Let this mind* be in you, which was also in Christ Jesus," who humbled Himself, laying aside His glory and condescending to our low estate; who became a servant, and took upon Him our burden, that the Father might be glorified in our salvation.*

There is no more solemn and comprehensive view of the Christian's life than that it is a mission. Christ sends us into the world as the Father sent Him. Christ, to fulfil the Father's mission, had to descend to the lowest depth of our misery; we, to fulfil Christ's mission, must by His very self-sacrifice be elevated to the height of union and communion with the risen Lord at the right hand of God. What unspeakable dignity is given to us, to be Christ's messengers, representatives, servants; to be the channels of His light, love, and power! And if in this mission, raised to Christ in the heavenly places, we have also to learn the fellowship of His sufferings, and to endure reproach for His name's sake, let us rejoice and give thanks that it is *given* to us on the behalf of Christ to suffer for His sake.†

5. Lastly, I would notice the persevering loyalty and the abounding fulness of Christ's life. The thought of the approaching night sometimes exerts a paralysing influence on man's energy and activity. It tempts us to anticipate our rest or to relax our effort. It often damps our enthusiasm.

* Phil. ii. 5. † Phil. i. 29; iii. 10.

We are inclined to think that we have laboured enough, and that we can add no more to our service, or to fear that our strength, our material, our opportunity, is exhausted. But Jesus was faithful to the end. As He approached the last sufferings in Jerusalem, His love and His zeal burned only with the greater intensity and brightness. To the very last, in His warnings to Judas, in His final addresses to the Jews, in the good confession which He confessed before Pontius Pilate, in His words to the daughters of Jerusalem, in His patient and silent suffering, and in the seven words from the cross—He fulfilled His ministry; He was faithful—the perfect Servant of God.

His love to His disciples was never more severely tested than during His last days. He never faltered. He never relaxed His faithful, anxious care of the men whom the Father had given Him to keep. He prayed for the disciples, anticipating the hour of temptation. On that night in which He was betrayed, and in which all the disciples were offended because of Him, Jesus manifested His love more fully than ever. He called them friends; He spoke to them of the love with which they are loved, of the vital union between the true vine and the branches; He instituted the memorial of His dying love; He prayed for them to His heavenly Father. In that prayer Jesus clings with the same love to the Father and to the disciples; and by the wonderful words, "I in them, and Thou in Me," He places believers in a position of glory, to which we can scarcely lift the eyes of our hearts. In the garden of Gethsemane He longed for the presence and sympathy of His disciples. When the evening came He protected them with the solicitude of a mother, so that no evil came near them. On His way to the judgment His merciful love looked upon Peter, and melted him to tears. No sorrow, pain, or trial could hinder Him from entering into the sorrow and need of others, or interrupt the outflowing of His love. He prayed on the cross for His enemies; He opened paradise to the robber, who appealed to His mercy; He remembered the desolateness of His mother Mary, and the affection of His favoured apostle. To the last moment He loved, to the last moment He was the Light of the world, until He entered into the three hours of darkness, when He wrought out atonement, and was made sin for us. The love which has no end, and which was stronger than death, is the love which had no beginning, eternal and divine, which has its origin in itself. It flows through the channel of Christ's humanity. As He loved, He loved to the end. To the very last moment He glorified the Father, and declared His name.

As the loyalty of Jesus was perfect, enduring to the end, so the measure of His obedience and work was without limit. Jesus never asked, "How *often* must I forgive, heal, bless?" He went about doing good. Only some of His marvellous works are recorded in the gospels. They give us the impression of incessant toil and labour, of constant and overflowing beneficence, of continued and abundant activity. In the gospel of Mark especially this aspect of Christ's life is brought before us. The word "straightway," "immediately," occurs very frequently. Here is presented to us the picture of a rapid and constant succession of labours. The works of Christ, as recorded in the gospel-narratives, are great in number and in variety. But they are only samples, selected by divine wisdom as representative works, in which His character, office, and salvation-power are manifested. The evangelist John tells us, "There are also many other things which Jesus did, the which, if they should be written every one, I suppose that even the world itself could not contain the books that should be written."* In what light

* John xxi. 25.

are we to view these innumerable works of which no record remains? Why did Jesus perform them? Simply because He was the Light of the world, and could not but shine forth with healing and peace; simply because He was love, because the Father dwelt in Him, because He said, "I must work the works of Him that sent Me. As long as I am in the world, I am the Light of the world." In this also we are called to follow Jesus. He is Lord, and we are His servants; He is infinitely great, and we are but little. But to the least of us the exhortation is addressed, "Be thou faithful unto death;" "Occupy till I come; work while—as long as—it is day." And to each one of us some peculiar talent is entrusted. We can be, we can do, we can suffer—something, and in some way, in which no other person can take our place.

As Jesus was the Light of the world, so are we in our measure and in our sphere. And in this mission or task there is no pause; as long as we are in the world it remains. There is no measure that we can say, "It is enough." The only measure is the daily opportunity appealing to the heart, out of which are the issues of life. Only let our heart be loving, and it will be like the measure Jesus describes, "Good measure, pressed down, and shaken together, and running over."

CHAPTER III.

The Example of Christ in the Light and Life of the Spirit.

"I am the Light of the world."—*John* viii. 12.

WE have dwelt on some characteristic features of our Lord's life. They are only a few drops from the ocean of light and love. In the life of Jesus there are not merely single moments and incidents which are beautiful; all is beautiful and perfect. We do not dwell so much on single features of His countenance, but, beholding Him, we see that He is fairer than the sons of men.

Jesus is the Light of the world; and as He commanded His disciples to let their light shine before men in such a manner that men may see their good works, and glorify the Father in heaven, who is the real but unseen fountain of their life, so Jesus Himself is to all mankind the manifestation of light; and even they who do not know who this Son of man is, acknowledge and feel the singular, the unique perfection and beauty of Jesus. In illustration of this remark, I would remind the reader of the oft-quoted observation of Rousseau, "that if Jesus had not really lived, the conception of such a character, as drawn in the narrative of the gospel, would itself be a miracle, a psychological problem, difficult to solve." The inventor, he says, would be greater than the hero himself. Jesus stands in history, but He is the miracle of history. Compare also the view of a great poet: "There appeared once upon earth an Individual, who by moral omnipotence only conquered far off ages, and founded an eternity of His own; who shone and attracted like a sun; who moved nations and centuries round the eternal and universal Centre. It is the quiet Spirit whom we call Jesus Christ. If He was, there is Providence, or He Himself is that Providence. Only gentle teaching and dying were the notes whereby this higher Orpheus tamed human beasts and turned rocks into cities. He, the purest among the mighty, the mightiest among the pure, lifted with His pierced hand empires out of their grooves, the stream of centuries out of its bed, and is still the Lord of the ages."*

* Jean Paul Richter.

Every reader of the gospel narrative must be impressed with the perfect harmony and unity of Christ's life. Thought and feeling, the inward life of contemplation and prayer, and the outward life of teaching and activity, are one. His life is but the manifestation of Himself. In all His words and works He stands before us with transparent clearness. We behold throughout the one Jesus, the Holy One of Israel. In Him we find strength and gentleness, meekness and zeal, wisdom and simplicity, courage and patience, indomitable purpose, inflexible firmness, and the most delicate sensitiveness—all masculine and all feminine excellencies perfectly blended, and that not by any effort, but as the outflow of one deep, central fountain of perfect holiness and uninterrupted communion with the Father. In Him we see the fulfilment of all God's commandments, the perfect realization of the divine idea of man. The temple is grand and vast. We see in Him the most marvellous variety and fulness of gifts, but the whole is filled with divine glory, with the Spirit in His sevenfold plenitude. All human feelings are in Him in so far as they are pure. Sometimes we see Him in childlike calmness and security—still and serene like a cloudless sky; sometimes burdened with thoughts of profoundest solemnity and sadness. Now He is placid, and the difficulties of His path and the opposition of men seem to make no impression on the strong rock; at other times He is most sensitive, feeling most keenly the latent hatred of His enemies; and in tears, and in words of burning indignation, the overwhelmed heart finds relief. He knows moments of joy, which, in the presence of His disciples, bursts forth in thanksgiving to the Father. Again He is exceeding sorrowful, and says to His three favoured disciples, "Tarry ye here, and watch with me." But at all times He is the same Jesus, abiding in the love of the Father. In solitude, in the circle of His disciples, in His teaching of the multitudes, in His dealings with the broken-hearted sinner and with the self-righteous scribes and Pharisees, in His temptations and sufferings, He presents to us the unity and harmony of perfect light, of perfect love.

We behold in Jesus not merely sinless, but perfect, all-sided, all-comprehensive humanity, tested by every kind of temptation and suffering. In the midst of the contradiction of sinners which He had to endure, the temptations of Satan and the world by which He was assailed, and the sorrow and agony which He had to bear, the perfection and strength of His love shone forth only with greater glory and more intense brilliancy. Jesus, and Jesus only, is "the Man," the representative of all humanity, the Son of man; and therefore He belongs to no nation or century, to no age or sex, to no peculiar calling and temperament. He is the Light of the world, the centre and magnet to draw all men unto Himself; He is the only One who can give out of His own fulness rest unto all who are weary, who is the all-sufficient guide, lover, and model of mankind.

Yet this is merely the outer view of the perfection of Christ. The Lord is in one sense intelligible and attractive to all men. The light shines forth. But when we behold the man Christ Jesus, we see Him, not merely *a* man, sinless and perfect, but the Son of man. The question He Himself, His very humanity, puts to us is, "*Who* is the Son of man?" And the answer which we give, taught by the Father, is, "He is the Son of God." And because (not although) He is the Son of God, He is the Son of man. Only David's Lord can be the promised Son of David; only man's Lord can be the Son of man. Jesus is not merely a member, but the Head of humanity, and that because He is the Only-begotten of the Father. No other solution can be given of this miracle of history, of "Pele" the Wonderful; no other explanation reaches the depth and height of this true Jacob's ladder; the very humanity and example of Jesus can only be comprehended in this light.

It has often been said that the life of Christ ceases to be an example to us when we regard the Saviour as the incarnate Son of God, and that His perfect purity and obedience would appeal more powerfully and effectually to our hearts, rousing our consciences and energising our wills, if we viewed Him as merely man.

In answer to this objection it might suffice to point out two facts. (1.) The true and real humanity of our Lord. He became like us in all things, sin excepted. In body, soul, and spirit He was man. He knew hunger and thirst, fatigue and exhaustion; He felt bodily pain and anguish. In thought and feeling He was true man. His temptations and conflicts were real. He gained the victory; not without pain, for He suffered being tempted; not without the putting forth of all His energy in faith, and by the remembrance of God's word. (2.) His was true human growth and development. The child Jesus grew not merely in stature, but in wisdom, and in favour with God and man. Christ, though the Son of God, *learned* obedience by the things which He suffered.

He grew up before God, and to His Father's delight.

Christ is therefore a real and perfect example to believers. We are called to walk as He walked in this world of sin, temptation, and suffering. The apostles, who constantly dwell on His divinity, bring before us the features of Christ's walk and obedience, and call upon us to walk in His footsteps, and to arm ourselves with the same mind. But their injunctions would be impracticable if Jesus was only perfect man.

For what sinful and fallen man needs is not man, however perfect, but *God*. He needs light, life, and love; and light, life, and love are divine, and can only come from above. The gift of God is His own Son. It is because Jesus is Light of light, the Son in the bosom of the Father, that He is the adequate, perfect, and ultimate revealer of God, the true and faithful Witness. No man knoweth the Father but the Son. It is only because Jesus is the eternal life, which was with the Father, that He is the source of life to all whom He quickens. The Word was made flesh, not that we might see the glory and perfection of humanity, (and how could sinful humanity bring forth that which is holy?) but that we should see the glory of the only-begotten God. The world seeing Jesus, exclaims, "Ecce Homo." The divine superscription and message is, "Say unto the cities of Judah, *Behold your God!*"

Again; we need not a repetition of the law, however perfect and glorious that exemplification of the law may be. Jesus is the embodiment of the divine law of love to God and man. This however only reveals our sin and confirms our condemnation. But the mission of Jesus lies in another and infinitely higher sphere. If a law could have been given which could give life, so the apostle Paul argued, Christ need not have come. We needed a new source of life, a second Adam, another root and beginning, so that transplanted into Him we might bring forth fruit unto God in newness of life. And this second Adam, though one with us, is not of us. He is the Lord from heaven. The child born unto us, the Son given unto us, is Immanuel, the mighty God. Jesus came not to restore us unto man's original condition of creaturely innocence, not to reinstate us into the position of the conditional covenant of law. He is *God's* righteousness for man. He came to give unto us the adoption of sons; to bring us into union with Himself, the true Vine, the Son of God. He died for us, and for us rose again, that He might be the quickening Spirit. He sends the Holy Ghost into our hearts, He gives us His own peace and joy, He works in us, and finally we are to be glorified together with Him. Divine righteousness, life, and glory are given to us in Christ Jesus. They could not be given to us by Him unless He is the Son of God; they could not actually be imparted to us except through the channel of His glorified humanity. It is only when we know the Son of God, the atoning death on the cross, and the glory of the heavenly High Priest, that we understand the meaning and realise the power of His example. And in the light of Christ's divinity we behold humanity invested with a dignity and glory of which we had no conception apart from the incarnation.

Our glory in and with Christ, our being conformed to the image of His Son—this was the eternal thought of God. In the first creation and in the dispensation of law we see the same idea shadowed forth, but not realised by reason of the creature's fallen and sinful condition. Man was created in the image of God. In the law given to sinful man everything was based upon the revelation of God: "I am the Lord thy God." "I am the Lord" was the reason of all precepts of humanity, of all kindliness and mercy to the poor and the blind, the weak and the helpless.

Israel was to be godly and God-like. "I am holy; be ye also holy." The standard as well as the remedy for man was not in humanity, but in God. In like manner Jesus commands men to love their enemies, to be forgiving and generous, not as the ideal of humanity, but that they may be the children of their Father which is in heaven. Unless man has a standard and source of righteousness above himself, he falls below himself—he is less than man. If Jesus was only perfect man, the Jehovahism of the Old Testament would be infinitely higher than Christianity. But Jesus is Jehovah, the fountain of living water. He is the incarnate Son of God, and gives unto us eternal life. He lifts us, who were lost sheep, high above the earthly pastures into His home, where we are loved with the infinite love which the Father had to Him. He condescends to make us members of His body; He promises to appoint unto us a kingdom, and to make us sharers of His glory; He has raised us above the holy angels who never fell, and we are called the Bride of the Lamb.

We read of our Lord, that, knowing that the Father had given all things into His hands, and that He was come from God and went to God, He rose and washed His disciples' feet. In the full consciousness of His glory, Jesus shows forth

His humility and love in ministering unto His disciples. In like manner it is because we know Jesus as our righteousness, life, and glory; because we know Him as He is now, exalted at the right hand of God, our Representative and High Priest; and because we hope to see Him, and to be like Him, that Christ in His whole earthly life is our manna; that we dwell on all His words and works; that we are exhorted to walk in love, as Christ also hath loved us. We return to the study of the Gospels in the light of the Pentecostal Epistles. Our position, attitude, and hope being heavenly, because Christ is in heaven, we are now called to walk in Christ's footsteps, and Christ Himself, by His Spirit, is the life and strength, as well as the light and standard of our walk.

Let us endeavour to place the same truth before the reader from the experimental point of view. We read of Jesus in the gospel narrative. We are impressed with the beauty and loveliness of His words and acts; we recognise in Him perfect purity and love. When we think of the man Christ Jesus, our first feeling is one of delight and joyous astonishment. We rejoice that Jesus belongs to our race, that such a perfect man lived on earth; we feel thankful that humanity has thus been represented and exalted.

But soon this joyous feeling gives way to one of sadness. When the example of Christ, the perfection of humanity, is presented to men that they may imitate and follow Him; when they are called to ascend the same lofty height, as if Jesus was the product, the efflorescence of our race, and as if there was in us also the same divine life and love, which only needs development, how utterly shallow and unprofitable does such teaching appear to the earnest and humble soul. For when we behold Jesus, the Son of man, and hear the testimony of the Father that He is well pleased in Him, we feel that we are not like Jesus, and that the holy and loving Father cannot be delighted with our hearts and lives. The image of Jesus wrings from our soul the exclamation: "Depart from me, for I am a sinful man, O Lord!" When we think of Jesus, we see the perfect illustration of David's word: "Behold, thou desirest truth in the inward parts: and in the hidden part thou shalt make me to know wisdom." When we think of ourselves, we feel the truth of David's confession in the same psalm: "Behold, I was shapen in iniquity; and in sin did my mother conceive me."* Jesus was spiritually minded; we are carnally minded. Jesus was from

---

* Psalm li. 5, 6.

above; we are of the earth, earthy. Jesus was good; but standing alone and viewing all men, even in their best aspect—their parental benevolence, He says to us all: "Ye who are evil." The sight of the man Christ Jesus rouses within us the consciousness of guilt, of sinfulness, and of our utter inability to be like Him. Can we ever be forgiven, and be brought into fellowship with the peace of Jesus? Can we ever be renewed, so as to be brought into fellowship with the mind of Jesus? Can we ever receive a new spirit, a new source of life, so as to be brought into fellowship with the life of Jesus?

Marvellous is the Scripture answer to these questions; marvellous both in substance and in its simplicity and unity.

Jesus, the Son of man, the servant of God, the beloved of the Father, is the Father's *gift* to poor sinful humanity. In the second part of the prophecy of Isaiah we find a strange combination of rebuke and consolation, of severe declaration of Israel's utter sin and helplessness, and heart-touching assurances of the divine favour and compassion. God tells His people that they are full of sin and ingratitude, that all His attempts to raise them have failed, that their hearts are full of idolatry, that Israel has destroyed itself. But when Israel had thus failed as a nation to be God's witness and servant in whom He can be glorified, God finds One who is in truth His servant, His elect, in whom His soul delighteth; One who in perfect, filial love is wholly devoted to His fear and service, who fully declares His name, who is anointed with the Spirit, and brings judgment unto victory by His meekness. God describes the perfection of this His servant, His faithfulness unto death, His sufferings borne without murmuring, and with most complete surrender to God's will. He expresses His love to this perfect One, His delight in Him, His perfect satisfaction with His work, and with His suffering. He dwells with joy on the reward which He will give unto Him for His obedience, and on the glory which shall follow His humiliation.

Now unto unfaithful and disobedient Israel God says: "This glorious One, in whom I delight, behold, I will give Him unto you; I will look upon Him as Israel, and I will look upon Israel as represented in Him. He is My covenant with you." He on whom the infinite love and delight of God rest, and whose obedience and suffering are infinitely pleasing to God, who declared perfectly God's name, and fulfilled His will, He is the gift of God to us; so that He is now our Lord and our representative. Now we understand what is implied in the joyous song, "Unto us a child is born, unto us a Son is given."* Jesus is God's unspeakable gift. He grew up before the Father, and the Father alone could fully understand the beauty of the life of Jesus; He alone could fathom the depth of the love with which Jesus loved. God beheld Jesus in His perfection, the only righteous One, in whose heart was God's law. God beheld the perfect obedience, victorious over all temptation, and loyal in all suffering. It was the Father's great delight, and will remain most precious to Him through all eternity. And this, His beloved Son, the Father gives unto us. As the righteous servant spoken of in Isaiah represented Israel before God, so we who accept the wonderful gift are regarded by God in Jesus.

Christ walked in love, and gave Himself an offering and a sacrifice to God for a sweet-smelling savour; God says it was *for us;* and the Father regards us now in Him with perfect satisfaction. The life and perfection of Jesus are not to witness against us, but for us. God sent Him, not to condemn us, but to save us; not to banish us into the depths of our guilt and sinfulness, but to elevate us into that home which He calls "My Father's

* Isaiah xlii. 6; ix. 6; lv. 4.

house," and in which we are to find our holy and peaceful abode.

But while this general declaration of the loving purpose of God in the gift and mission of Jesus kindles within us hope, it is only in the cross of Christ that we can see clearly the method of our acceptance, salvation, and renewal. If Jesus had only lived, we should possess only the *record* of His life, but not *His life itself.* He gave us His life when He poured out His soul unto death, when He shed His blood for the remission of sins. True, God gave His Son from eternity; at Bethlehem; during the years of Christ's ministry; but the actual giving of the Son was when the Father gave Him up, when He made Him who knew no sin to be sin for us. It is only by the death of Jesus that the Lord becomes Jehovah-Tsidkenu. The glorious links "together with Christ" begin only on the cross. There the Shepherd has found the lost sheep, never to be separated from it. We do not read that we were born together with Christ at Bethlehem, or tempted together with Christ in the wilderness. The meeting-place of Christ and the sinner is on Calvary. We have been crucified together, buried together, and raised together with Christ; we are seated together with Him in heavenly places. When the poor and needy sinner comes to Jesus as the Saviour, all the three questions are solved together. We have redemption in Christ, even the forgiveness of sins; and in that forgiveness we possess righteousness apart from works. When God forgives us all the transgressions of His law for Christ's sake, He regards us as having fulfilled all the law in the same Christ;* and we are the righteousness of God in Him. And in the forgiveness of sins God renews the heart and sends forth the Spirit of His Son. We become thus partakers of the peace, the mind, and the life of Christ. When we believe in Jesus, we are justified, we are renewed, we are filled with the Spirit. It is this self-same faith in the Lord our Righteousness by which we are throughout our earthly life sanctified and kept unto the perfect salvation.

The following Scriptures bring before us the simplicity of God's method.

The expression of the highest Christian life is, in the words of the apostle Paul, "I have been crucified with Christ: nevertheless I live; yet not I, but Christ liveth in me." No higher experience or attainment is possible for us. Separated from his guilt, from the world, and from his sinful self, by the cross of Jesus, the apostle knows that the

* Augustine.

Son of God Himself dwells in his heart, and that He is the source and strength, as well as the object and joy, of his life. As he has been brought into death, so he has also been quickened by the Spirit of the risen Saviour, the second Adam. But how is Paul able to say this of himself? It is by faith. But by what faith? By that same elementary faith by which he first appropriated Jesus as his righteousness, and by no other. "For the life which I now live in the flesh I live by faith in the Son of God, who loved me, and gave Himself for me."*

"Jesus dwells in our hearts by faith." This is the most beautiful and attractive description of the Christian condition. The Lord was once a stranger to us; then we heard His voice, and saw His glory; then, perhaps after many doubts and struggles, we were brought to submit ourselves to the righteousness of God, and to receive the grace which bringeth salvation to the chief of sinners. But now Jesus has made His abode with us. According to His gracious promise, Jesus is now permanently and continuously dwelling in our heart with His peace, His love, and with all the treasures of His grace. And how is this? By faith. By what faith? Certainly not by faith

* Gal. ii. 20, 21.

in *Christ in us*, but by faith in Christ for us; by that self-same fundamental faith in Jesus, crucified for sinners, and raised again, by which we were first accepted and justified; by that initial faith through which grace saved us.

The description of his attitude which the apostle Paul gives in the epistle to the Philippians is also full of instruction. He acknowledges that he has not yet "already attained, either were already perfect." He was pressing forward "toward the mark for the prize of the high calling of God in Christ Jesus." The perfection which stood before his heart was above, heavenly and future. It will be reached by us when Christ shall appear, and change the bodies of our humiliation, that they may be fashioned like unto His glorious body. Then shall we bear the image of the heavenly; then shall we be like Him, for we shall see Him as He is. Our perfection is given us when we are glorified together with Christ; when the end of our predestination is attained, and we are conformed to the image of His Son.

To be content with any other perfection, with any (imagined) annihilation or cleansing of the flesh, is contrary to the word of God, leading to self-deception, and beguiling us from the simplicity of the gospel. While we are on earth sin is in us; the flesh warreth against the Spirit, the Canaanite is always in the land. We are not like Jesus, who, although tempted in all things as we are, was yet without sin—in whom there was no principle of enmity against God and His holy will. But although our perfection is above in Christ, the knowledge of Christ and our faith in Him influence us in our walk below. Although our perfection is future, at the coming of our Saviour, the hope of being like Christ influences us at present; for every one that hath this hope purifieth himself, even as Christ is pure. Our conscience is purged from dead works by the blood of Christ, and thereby we are enabled to serve God. Though we know that we are in the flesh, we are not to walk after the flesh; but because the Spirit of Christ dwelleth in us, we are spiritually-minded, and fight the good fight of faith.*

What then is the apostle's striving while he looks forward to the perfection in body, soul, and spirit at Christ's coming? It is to cast away continually his own righteousness, which is of the law, that he may win Christ, and be found in Him, having the righteousness which is through the faith of Christ, the righteousness which is of God

---

* 1 John iii. 2; Rom. viii. 9, 10.

by faith. He was therefore continually looking to that very *Jesus for us*, our righteousness, to whom he looked at his conversion. And it was by the exercise of *this* faith that he grew in the knowledge of Christ, and of the power of His resurrection and the fellowship of His sufferings, being made conformable unto His death, while the hope of the resurrection of the just animated and strengthened him to run the race set before him.*

When Christians feel that their spiritual life is languid, that they have left their first love, and that they are not overcoming sin and the world, they are tempted to look for some new starting-point, and imagine that they need some other kind of faith than that first faith which rested in Jesus for the forgiveness of sin and acceptance with the Father. But "other foundation can no man lay than that is laid." God says that among His people none will say, "I am sick,"† for they shall all have forgiveness of sin. Why then do we, when we are weak, seek any other remedy?

Wherever forgiveness of sin is, Luther often said, there is life and blessedness. It is our experience that whenever we have a vivid sense of our pardon, the heart is full of peace and love, the spirit feels strong, joyous, and of good courage;

* Phil. iii. 8–21.   † Isaiah xxxiii. 24.

we are humble, tender, and compassionate; we look forward with hope to the future, and engage in our work with liberty and cheerful energy. We feel the presence of the indwelling Spirit, and a sweet sense of the Father's love, and of Jesus as our own Lord and Saviour. If this be true, then, whenever we are weak, gloomy, desponding, murmuring against God's leadings, disinclined to do the work before us, is it not because there is some obscuration of that central point, *the forgiveness of sins?* The reason may be that we deem some sins small and unimportant, and do not confess them before the Lord; we do not bring them into the light of the throne of grace, we do not condemn ourselves before God, and therefore we carry, as it were, the burden of these sins, and their shadow darkens our heart. When we make no progress in our Christian path, when the spiritual life is sick and feeble, it is to the central point we must turn, *Christ for us.* There alone can we find renewal of repentance, of godly sorrow, of love, of joy, and of strength. Sin need not drive us away from the throne of grace; but the grace which pardons our sin drives us from the love and bondage of sin.

We have redemption in Christ; redemption is a comprehensive word, including deliverance from all our enemies, and yet the apostle explains it by adding, the forgiveness of sins.*

God is the source of all good; and the knowledge of God and of Jesus Christ is eternal life. But this is the knowledge of the Father and of the Son, to behold in Christ crucified that God is love. In this God is manifested, that Christ is the propitiation for our sins. Hence to study in our hearts this article of the remission of sins, is to acquaint ourselves with God.

The difficulty which the apostle Paul seems to have felt with all his congregations, was to convince them of the perfection of Christ, and of the all-sufficiency, simplicity, and comprehensiveness of the gospel of grace. Our tendency is first to lower Christ, and then to feel the necessity for something in addition to this self-made conception of the Saviour. "Come to Jesus," is the first message to the sinner; it continues to be the divine message to the believer. Jesus is our righteousness, our life, and the hope of glory. Our great and lifelong task is to abide in "the simplicity that is *into Christ*."†

In humble and joyous faith in the Lord Jesus, in whom we are complete, let us contemplate His whole life on earth; let us listen to His word: "I

---

* Eph. i. 7.   † 2 Cor. xi. 3 (original).

must work the works of Him that sent Me, as long as it is day." Only they who have been reconciled to God by Christ's death can be saved by His life; only they who have been begotten again by His resurrection, can follow His example. In the outer circle of Christendom, the real essence and nature of Christianity is not known. Christianity, as opposed to the spirit of the world, as contrasted with the preparatory and intermediate dispensation of the old covenant, does not consist in opinions and principles; it is the life which, through the blood of Christ and the indwelling of the Holy Ghost, is given unto all who believe in Jesus. This is what the apostles always put before their congregations. Hence they never speak of Christianity, of principles, of endeavours, but of Christ, who for us died and rose again; who hath brought us all spiritual blessings, gifts, and powers; who dwelleth in our hearts by faith; by whom strengthening us we can do all things; and who shall finally present us unblameable in body, soul, and spirit, before the Father. The grace of God bringeth salvation, and in this grace we stand.

When we think of apostolic Christianity, do we not sometimes feel as if we had not begun yet to be Christians—as if we were still, so to speak, the disciples of John the Baptist, and had not yet received the Spirit? Let us then again, and daily, lift up our eyes to the Lord, and behold Jesus at the right hand of God, in whom we have the Father's love, and from whom we receive the Holy Ghost. Let us, born again as we are of incorruptible seed, be daily renewed in our mind; let us learn Christ. The example of Christ is given unto believers that they may constantly and stedfastly study it; that they may daily, with full purpose, walk in His footsteps. As we rest in the promises, and give thanks for the position which grace has assigned to us, so it is ours to put on the Lord Jesus day by day, to appropriate by prayer and meditation, in watchfulness and self-restraint, the words of Christ. His words include all the teaching of His earthly walk. Only they are true branches in Christ who are disciples, that is learners, who patiently and earnestly listen to the Master, and obey His commandments; who exercise themselves unto godliness, and accept meekly the correction of His Spirit and the chastening of His hand. If we have received the Spirit our life-long study and delight will be the example of Jesus, as it is recorded in the gospels.

CHAPTER IV.

The Unity of our Life, and its Relation to Eternity.

"While it is day: the night cometh, when no man can work."
John ix. 4.

HUMAN life has been illustrated in Scripture by numerous and various metaphors. Viewing it in its beauty and organic development, as well as in its frailty, Scripture sees the type of human life in the flower of the field, which to-day flourisheth, and to-morrow "the wind passeth over it and it is gone; and the place thereof shall know it no more." Moses, the servant of God, watching the unsubstantial and unprofitable character of much of our life, noticing during the long journeying through the wilderness how many days and weeks passed away in mere existence, calls life a sleep and "a tale that is told."

Looking at the busy plans and projects of man, formed with as great ease and hopefulness as they are rapidly disappointed, the epistle of James speaks of life as "a vapour, that appeareth for a little time and then vanisheth away."*

Again, life is likened to a pilgrimage; on which God's people go "from strength to strength," until at last they appear before Him in Zion. Our Saviour likens it to a twofold road; and while the wide gate has ushered many, without any thought or effort, into the broad road, which leadeth unto destruction, the Lord calls upon men to enter in at the strait gate, and to join the few who are journeying unto eternal blessedness.†

Again, life is compared with a warfare; for man is constantly in conflict with difficulties, with enemies and hostile influences; or, still sadder, he is at enmity with God, resisting His dealings and forsaking with great effort his own mercies. ‡ Hence the apostle speaks of a good or beautiful fight, that of faith, in which all are conquerors and crowned with unfading glory. He speaks also of a race in which no impure and selfish ambition is the motive or sustaining power, but love to the

---

* Ps. ciii. 15, 16; xc. 9; James iv. 14.
† Ps. lxxxiv. 7; Matt. vii. 13, 14.
‡ Jonah ii. 8.

Lord who has called us, and in which we strive "for the prize of the high calling of God in Christ Jesus."*

But of all illustrations the comparison of human life with a day seems the most beautiful, because in the simplest, yet most accurate and touching manner, it describes not merely life, but also the consciousness of life; not merely the outward changes and developments, but also the inward feelings with which we pass through our earthly course.† The metaphor describes both the objective and subjective aspect of life. The early morning is not merely like childhood, but it recalls the feeling we had as children; and when we review in imagination the various aspects of the day from morn to even, we are reminded not merely of the characteristic events and occupations, but also of the characteristic tone and feeling of the various ages of man. The morning, mysterious, fragrant, and full of promise; the early hours of the day, bright, strong, capacious; the fulness of light and

---

* 1 Tim. vi. 12; Heb. xii. 1, 2.

† The ancient Egyptians have a symbolic narrative combining the life-path of man and the day-path of the sun. "The sun completes his course by appearing in the heavens while it is day, first as a child, then as a youth, and at last as an old man."—EBERS, *Ægypten und Moses*.

warmth, vigour and energy, of midday; the cheerful and fruit-bearing hours of the afternoon; the subtle, scarcely perceptible, change when it is towards evening; the calm and solemn evening—all this is easily translated into the various phases of our life-consciousness. From childhood to old age is like a day; and we pass through the various feelings of morning, noon, and evening. And at last comes the night. Who does not understand and feel the force of the petition—

> "Teach me to live that I may dread
> The grave as little as my bed."

Our life is like a day. Mysterious is the day-spring from which it took its rise; full of awe and darkness seems the night to which it hastens; and the short hours between appear full of sorrow and hardship. "I know not whence I came, I know not whither I go, I know not how I can be so cheerful," was the inscription on one tombstone, and the secret language of thousands of wayfarers. The ancients were oppressed with the sense of human misery. The problems of life, with its conflicts and sorrows, its partings and losses, its short-lived smiles and joys, and the long-enduring and corroding effects of grief and disappointment, form the burden of their meditations and complaints.* In Scripture also God allows men, and even His saints, to express all the sad, bitter, and overwhelming feelings of the heart in the midst of the trials and dark labyrinthine paths of life. In the book of Job, in the writings of the royal preacher, in the Psalms, and in the Lamentations of Jeremiah, this aspect of life is most fully described. God permits us to look into the very hearts of His saints. The thoughts and feelings which in their sore trial and anguish overwhelm their souls, leading them close to the borders of the land of unbelief and despair; the questions and doubts which rise in their minds, and which they cannot bury, but, in the intensity of their grief and of their real clinging to God, must express in His presence; the sorrow which refuses to be comforted, and seems to be an inexhaustible fountain of tears—all this is brought before us in language so sincere and strong that we can at first sight scarcely distinguish it from the sadness of the

---

* Homer speaks of man as the most miserable being on earth, whom the gods appointed to live a life of sighs. (*Iliad*, xvii. 446; xxiv. 525.) Another ancient sentence says men were created out of the tears of the gods. The remark, that the best thing for man would be never to be born, the next best thing to die as quickly as possible, became almost proverbial. (Occurs also in Soph. *Œd. Col.*) Man is but the shadow of a dream, says Pindar.

world, which has no hope. Scripture records these deep soul-trials for our consolation and encouragement, lest we think it a strange thing when we fall into divers temptations, or fear that murmuring and dejection such as ours can never be forgiven and healed by divine grace.

But neither Israel nor the Church of Christ look upon life with despondency, or in any other light than that of thanksgiving and praise. It is because we believe in redemption that we are able to thank God for our creation. It is because we look forward to the glory of eternity, and because we possess the means of grace, that our life-day, though full of trouble and sorrow, discipline and conflict, is also full of light and strength. In the love of God, which spared not His own Son, we have the pledge of His Fatherly providence guiding our steps, and making all things work together for good. In the constant experience that God hears our voice and supplication we renew our joyous resolution, "I will call upon Him as long as I live." The end, we know, is life everlasting, and the whole path is irradiated by our hope. The children of God never meet in the presence of God without praise. There is a deep under-current of joy and gladness in their souls; they make melody in their hearts. Although

Jacob in one sense mourns, "Few and evil have been the days of my pilgrimage," the same patriarch confesses, "I am not worthy of the least of Thy mercies;" nor did the hope disappoint him which he cherished all his life, and which on his death-bed interrupted, as his deepest pent-up feeling, his inspired predictions, "I have earnestly waited for Thy salvation." *

But there is yet another source of strength and consolation, of gladness and heartsease, to us Christians, children of the new covenant. In this our day-path, in this our day-labour, we have the presence of Jesus, our Immanuel. We rejoice that He passed through infancy and childhood, that He knew the life of youth and manhood, that He sanctified every age, and that He made every part of the path luminous. As He left us a perfect example, so He possesses now perfect and all-developed sympathy with us in work and in rest, in sorrow and in joy, in temptation and in suffering, in loneliness and in the fellowship with man. It is the sympathy and the spiritual presence of our Lord Jesus Christ which vitalises to us all that is recorded of Him and His walk on earth; so that it is to us nourishing bread and cheering wine, that it shines on our path and makes our steps

* Gen. xlvii. 9; xlix. 18.

safe, that thereby we have communion with the man Christ Jesus, and feel that He is actually living and walking with us day by day. It is out of this living treasury of His earthly experience He has given us this word also: "I must work the works of Him that sent Me, as long as it is day."

The life of Jesus was indeed a perfect day; His path was that of the Just One, shining more and more, and His sunset was full of unspeakable glory. Our life is fragmentary; and that is one of the most painful feelings of the disciple, that in his life there is so much failure. Grace has won but scanty triumphs; many lovely flowers and promising buds have seen no fulfilment, and matured in no fruit; numerous, heavy, and irreparable are the sins of omission; many sins, errors, and self-chosen paths, have injured and impoverished his life. And yet in all this the Christian is upheld by faith in God. Among all nations there has been a deep-seated belief in an overruling providence. Among the ancients, providence appeared more in the form of necessity; a hidden yet ruling righteousness and all-adjusting power. Among modern nations, even the most superficial knowledge of scripture has confirmed and ennobled this idea.

> "There's a Divinity that shapes our ends,
> Rough-hew them how we will."

Were this saying quoted a million times, unless a million times experience made a new application of this truth?

But on the territory of revelation we see clearly light. When we are brought into the sanctuary, the thoughts and difficulties which perplexed and well-nigh overwhelmed us find their consoling solution. God knows our path even in the midst of our confused wanderings. As we pray, "Guide us with thy counsel," we add the certain and all-blessed end—"and receive us to glory." Notwithstanding all our sins and errors, He brings us to our desired haven. Israel is chastened, but led by infinite wisdom and mercy; for He heals their backslidings. The wickedness of Joseph's brethren is overruled for their salvation. Our folly, our waywardness, our continual retrograde movements, our sinfulness, cannot frustrate His wisdom, mercy, patience, and love. He is God, and His glory will ultimately shine forth in the full and abundant salvation of His people. Each child of God will have his own name; the result of all his earthly experience, and divine education.

In deep humility and in reverent trustfulness

the Old Testament language is: "I know that it is not in man that walketh to direct his steps."* And again: "Thou hast taught me from my youth .... I will yet praise thee more and more."† And when Jesus came, He declared the Father-name of God. He, the only-begotten from all eternity; He, the first-begotten of the dead, the firstborn among many brethren, now leads us to His God and our God, to His Father and our Father. When He speaks of the future, He says: "In My Father's house are many mansions;" and His Father's house is also ours, where He prepares a place for us. If we confess Him before men, He will also confess us before *His* heavenly Father. He promises us that during this earthly life His Father will watch over us, and shelter us under His protecting care; even as for the sake of man *our* Father cares for the sparrows, and not one of them can fall to the ground without His will.‡

The high point of view from which the New Testament regards the comforting doctrine of providence is, that we are purchased with Christ's blood, and identified with Him now as sons of

---

* Jeremiah x. 23. † Psalm lxxi. 17, 14.
‡ Matt. x. 29, 32. Compare "*your* Father" and "*my* Father."

God and heirs of glory, and on our way to heaven. Shall not God with Christ give us all things, and in this only complete the work and purpose of grace?

In this highest light all the apostolic teaching places the comforting truth, "He careth for you." Our whole life is viewed under the aspect of sanctification; of leading us heavenward; of furnishing us unto every good work, and sustaining us in every conflict; of performing in us the good work which grace has begun, and bringing us faultless into the presence of His glory. The chain which begins in predestination and ends in glory cannot be broken. Whom He justified He also glorified. Between these two links lies the all-wise and merciful guidance of our steps during our earthly pilgrimage.*

If the Old Testament saint, on the same basis of eternal and unchangeable, sovereign and almighty love, was able to say, "The Lord will perfect that which concerneth me: thy mercy, O Lord, endureth for ever: forsake not the works of Thine own hands"†—with what fuller clearness and joyousness can the new covenant children say, "We know that all things work together for good

---

* Romans viii. 30, compare with 1 Peter i. 3–9.
† Psalm cxxxviii. 8.

to them that love God, to them who are the called according to His purpose."*

The life of God's people is thus, notwithstanding all their sins and errors, made a unity by the love of our Saviour-God. Look at the records of Scripture which we possess of some lives, traced from their very early morning to the night. How brief, simple, clear, and loving the God-appointed course seems to us now; how tardy, enigmatic, difficult, and trying it appeared to them as they journeyed onwards. Think of Samuel, the last of the judges and the first of the prophets. What a long, continuous, useful, laborious life was his! The burden of the nation rested upon him; for many years he was the father and ruler of the people. Through him the word of God came unto Israel; he established the school of the prophets. The same servant of God who as a child had announced to Eli the impending judgment, anointed David, the son of Jesse, according to God's command. During all these years of meditation, work, and service, Samuel walked with God—a man of fervent prayer and priestly intercession, a man of earnest faith and burning love. In answer to his prayer thunder and rain came down in the midst of the wheat har-

* Romans viii. 28.

vest; for his was the prayer of faith, the prayer of one who lived in communion with God, and belonged to the true Israel who prevail with the Lord. Strong as his faith was his love. The nation's ingratitude could never quench the fire of his loving intercession. "God forbid that I should cease to pray for you." Samuel's life is like a long noble river, and we can trace it to its very source. Samuel was yet a tender youth when all Israel, even from Dan to Beersheba, perceived that God was with him, and that he was established to be a prophet of the Lord, and that God did let none of his words fall to the ground. It was the revelation of God in that memorable night, when in the silent sanctuary he heard the mysterious voice which was the beginning of Samuel's prophetic life. Still further back we see him in Shiloh ministering "before the Lord, being a child, girded with a linen ephod," spending a few bright, quiet years in the service of the sanctuary, and under the training of Eli. On the well-known and longed-for day we see Hannah appear with her husband to offer the yearly sacrifice, bringing a little coat, with her motherly benediction and kisses. Nay, even before Samuel had opened his eyes to the light of the world, his whole life and ministry had been the subject of Hannah's earnest supplication, and of God's loving and gracious promise.

Look again at the life of John the Baptist. It lies before us from its very commencement to the end. How perfect, yet how brief; how sad, and yet how glorious it was. He was a man sent from God, chosen to be the forerunner of the Most High; the child of many prayers, announced by the angel Gabriel; sanctified by the Holy Ghost even from his mother's womb. The morning hours of a father's faithful teaching, and a mother's tenderness; a few years of meditation in the word of God in the wilderness; a few years of bright and burning testimony, like the sun in mid-day splendour; and the death of a martyr—such was the short, but glorious day of this chosen one, this highly-favoured messenger of the King!

While in the case of Samuel and the Baptist the unity of life appears most strikingly in the continuity of their spiritual life from its commencement, the life of the apostle Paul presents a somewhat different aspect. When he looks back on his past life he is able to view the long course of his discipleship, his ministry, his apostolic work, and his Christian fight, as one. But though the previous part of his earthly life was in unbelief, and without the knowledge of Christ, spent even in persecuting the Church, the apostle, who ever confesses and laments his past sin, yet looks on his whole past life as under the guidance and power of divine love. Going back to his very birth, and to his descent from Israel, he says, "It pleased God, who separated me from my mother's womb, and called me by His grace;"* and again, "God, whom I serve from my forefathers with pure conscience."† We can also trace the divine wisdom preparing the apostle for his great work by his experience as a Pharisee, and arranging the events of his youth, his education, and his Roman citizenship, so as especially to fit him for his subsequent grand mission. In many other saints we can trace this unity of the Lord's dealings with them, even before they knew Him. This is true not only of men like the apostle Paul and Luther, but of every child of God. Divine grace makes the life of His children one day. He loved us before we knew Him. Out of the uncreated eternal light we hear a voice, "I have loved thee with everlasting love; therefore with loving-kindness have I drawn thee."

Not all who are born into this world are permitted to live the whole day of life. Night comes often before evening, nay, even earlier. Abruptly, and to us mysteriously, the brief morning hours are

* Gal. i. 15. † 2 Tim. i. 3.

terminated by the advent of death. Yet the life of God's children is always perfect and complete. So we have seen it in the case of John the Baptist; so it was with the proto-martyr Stephen, in whose angelic countenance all that is lovely in human life shone forth—the transparent simplicity of childhood, the ideal ardour of youth, the heroism and strength of manhood, and the reflective calmness and mercifulness of old age. How many thousands of children stand before the throne of God, called away in the early morning to the land of rest. Infants, who have scarcely seen the light of our sun, now behold the more glorious light of eternity; they who have but uttered the cry of feebleness and pain, sing now glory to God and to the Lamb; they who have only felt without understanding it the affection of earthly parents, are now drinking from the river of divine love. Foremost among them we behold the babes of Bethlehem, who offered their tiny bosoms to shield the infant Jesus, and instead of Him received the mortal wound. They rest now in the bosom of Jesus. To them was given the rest of Paradise, though they had scarcely known the land of banishment, and after the briefest conflict they are crowned with the martyr's crown.*

* O parvuli beati, modo nati, nondum tentati, nondum luctati, jam coronati.—*Augustine.*

The death of infants brings before us in a solemn and impressive manner the depth of our fall; it reminds us how sin having entered into the world, death has come to all the branches, and even the most tender buds. But it is as if the tender love of our heavenly Father intended to make death less awful and painful to us by associating with it little infants, whom for the sake of the second Adam and in the divine garment of His righteousness He transplants into His paradise. They will be in heaven members of the mystical body of Christ. Their's is not angelic innocence and purity. Christ is their righteousness. Their robes also are made white in the Blood of the Lamb. Linked to us by the sweet and sacred tie which God the Creator has established, and by the bond of a special affection, they will present an aspect of divine grace and of the glory of Christ and His work which no other human beings or angels can manifest. They will in a peculiar manner show forth the wonders of redeeming grace and of the Spirit's power. And then shall we look upon their earthly life as complete; and they also shall belong to the saints of God, who can say, "The Lord hath perfected that which concerneth me."

In the light of the eternal love of God we behold the unity of the life of His children; in the light of the relation which subsists between our present and our everlasting existence the solemnity of our life-day.

Our life-day is short; but viewed in the light of eternity, it possesses an intensive depth, and cannot be measured by the length of its duration. Unless eternity was written on the heart of man he would have no consciousness of the brevity of his life, or mourn over its limits and fetters. The very misery of man bespeaks the grandeur which he has lost. However "far inland" he may be, and however determined to shut out the thought of a Hereafter-eternity—he cannot divest even the present life of its spiritual, eternal, and solemn character. In every human affection, in tears and in smiles, in the beauty of nature around us, in all our thoughts, when we are most truly communing with ourselves God meets us, and we are reminded that we are His offspring. How true is the testimony of the German poet: "When man under the clouds of life casts from him his fortune, because he thinks it of less value than his heart, he is as blessed and great as the beatified spirits above. And we are worthy of a holier earth, because the view of sacrifice elevates instead of depressing us, and we shed burning tears, not out of pity, but out of profoundest, holiest, love and joy." We are fallen and in bondage, but we cannot lower our nature, our dignity, our inalienable birthright; our nature is to live with God, for Him and in Him, and hence for evermore.

And who of us, in his inmost heart, would willingly consent to be but the creature of Time, and to disappear after the brief day of our earthly existence? Are we so satisfied with the broken cisterns, which can hold no water, that we can utterly forget the fountain of eternal life? Are we so satisfied with the fare which is earned with toil and degrading bondage in the strange country that we have no longing for the native land of our spirits? Are we ready to sell the birthright of our immortality for the enjoyment of even Time's noblest gift?

Yet even if we succeeded in dehumanizing ourselves, and were content with a mere earthly intellectual existence, apart from God and without the hope of eternity, we cannot find the land in which it is always afternoon; we cannot stay the setting sun; and the true character of our life and destiny must at last be revealed to us with irresistible clearness.

Eternity is before us. At present it is only by an effort of the imagination, or, in the case of the Christian, by the exercise of faith, that we realise the spiritual and everlasting world. Of those divine realities which are unseen and hoped for, faith is the substance and evidence. To the unbeliever it seems very vague; to the Christian even it seems sometimes very far off. But how often have we experienced, on a smaller scale, that what at one time seemed a distant object of imagination, hope, or fear—at last came into actual existence! Then we say "it is," and it is the past which appears a dream and a shadow. In like manner, when our life-day is past, when the night cometh, then eternity will be no longer merely imagined or dimly anticipated by faith, but the actual consciousness and experience of the soul.

Our life-day, however, does not merely precede our eternity. It is connected with eternity by the more inward and solemn sequence of seed-time and harvest, of germ and maturity. As our life is one, and forms an unity, so its result is stereotyped at death for evermore. Out of our life-day is born our everlasting blessedness or misery, our everlasting fellowship with God and conformity with Christ, or our everlasting separation from God and the light of His countenance. On earth, and here only, can we sow. "He that soweth to his flesh shall of the flesh reap corruption; but he that soweth to the Spirit shall of the Spirit reap life everlasting." *

It is this tremendous and everlasting issue which is decided by our acceptance or rejection of the gospel, and which remains fixed at the time of our death. Thus our blessed Lord Himself preached the joyous yet awful gospel, and thus He commissioned His messengers to set before men the only way of salvation. "He that believeth on the Son hath everlasting life: and he that believeth not the Son ... the wrath of God abideth on him." Christ's own solemn warnings, in which He exhorts us to make even the most painful sacrifice of a right hand and a right arm, are based on the awful and the fixed ultimate destiny of those who reject His love and authority.† As throughout His ministry, so, if possible, with greater solemnity in His closing words on Olivet. Who can evade the plain meaning of His majestic words, "Then shall He say also unto them on the left hand, Depart from Me, ye cursed, into everlasting fire, prepared for the devil and his angels?" or who can disturb the fearful equality of duration implied in His concluding sentence: "And these shall go into everlasting punishment: but the righteous

---

* Galatians vi. 8.
† John iii. 36; Matthew v. 29, 30.

Our Life: its Relation to Eternity.

into life eternal"?* And when the apostles and their followers brought the divine message to men, they were impressed and well-nigh overwhelmed with the alternative which was thus through them placed before immortal souls—eternal life or everlasting death.

This is so clearly the tenor of the New Testament, as indeed it was also the doctrine of the Old,† and so little dependent on single expressions, that all Christendom has given forth the solemn message.

Some speculative minds, and among them some very devout and loving ones, have in all ages of the Church endeavoured to reach beyond what is written, or to explain the statements of Scripture so as to either teach the ultimate restoration of all, or the annihilation of the wicked. But Scripture holds out no prospect of the gospel being preached in the next world, and if preached, of its being accompanied with renewing power. It addresses itself simply to the hearers of the gospel, and

* Matt. xxv. 12, 30, 41, 46. The same word αἰώνιον used in both cases.

† In the New Testament the manifestation of Christ brought with it much clearer and fuller disclosures of eternal life and death, of the world of angels, and of Satan. But the germ of the doctrine spoken of is in many passages, such as Ps. i. 4; xi. 6, 7; Dan. xii. 2, 3; Mal. iii. 17; iv. 1.

places before them blessedness and glory in words of the brightest and loftiest character, or anguish and darkness in terms strong and appalling. Jesus speaks of those who are cast out, even though they belonged to the household of God; but neither He nor His apostles ever say that any shall be brought in again and restored out of that "outer darkness," where there is "weeping and gnashing of teeth."* The apostle Paul speaks of those who obey not the gospel of our Lord, that they "shall be punished with everlasting destruction from the presence of the Lord." And in the last page of the Apocalypse, the furthest glimpse vouchsafed unto us into the ages to come, is there a single ray of hope held out for the unbelievers who have been judged, or a single word to encourage the idea that the judgment of God is not final, and that the two classes remain distinct and separate for ever, the just and the unjust, the purified ones and those who are defiled with sin? In the same chapter which describes the glories of the New Jerusalem, and the eternal joy of the saints who inherit all things, we read that all that do iniquity "have their part" (fearful antithesis to the inheritance) "in the lake which burneth with fire and brimstone: which is the second death."

* Matt. viii. 11, 12.

The same inspired words which reveal to us the blessedness of the redeemed, bring before us the dark and ultimate destiny of those that are "without."* If we accept the testimony of Scripture, there is a conclusion of history; there is a judgment, beyond which there is no change; after which there is neither the conversion nor the annihilation of immortal spirits, but the endless continuance of the second death.

There are many analogies in our human life and experience which bring before us the thought, that a point of time arrives in which dangers, remedies, opportunities, which were possible, accessible, and effective, are beyond all reach. Why may the Bible statements concerning the future irreversible sentence, "Too late, too late," not be founded in the very nature of things, as well as the character and will of God? The great theosoph Böhme says: "Here in this life the soul is in the balance, and can be born again in love; when the beam is broken, the soul is in her own land, in her ground-element" (*Principio*).

Speculations beyond and apart from, as well as contrary to, Scripture (though by God's grace they may not injure materially some of their authors), exert a most injurious influence on the

* 2 Thess. i. 9; Rev. xxi. 8; xxii. 11–15.

great mass of mankind. These are only too willing to accept anything that will blunt the edge of the gospel message, and furnish them with excuses (however illogical) for negligence and delay. Such views cannot fail to affect the very character of the gospel message itself—the views which we hold of God, of sin, of the death of Christ. Nor, it is to be feared, do even orthodox Christians and Christian ministers altogether escape the weakening influence of the prevalence of such opinions. We breathe the atmosphere and unless we are on our guard we are affected by it.

It is impossible for us to speak with too profound humility or too great tenderness. But if we remember from what Christ has saved us, even from everlasting ruin, (*and was not this our consciousness at our conversion?*) and if we truly love the souls of men, we shall not be influenced by the shallow criticism which would banish the presentation of the wrath of God and everlasting misery from our teaching and from our evangelistic addresses. He who loved as never man loved, who wept over Jerusalem, who died on the cross, has Himself given us the example, as well as the commission, to lay before men life and death.

If such is the connection between life and eternity, and if the night may set in at any moment in childhood, in youth, or at any part of our subsequent course, how blessed is it that the grace of God can bring unto us salvation at all times and at any time—that from early morn to the eleventh hour* the Lord calls us to enter into His kingdom, and into the service of love which is crowned with an everlasting reward. God is able to renew the infant heart, and His Holy Spirit, in a way which we cannot comprehend, can graft infants into the true vine, so that in death they fall asleep in Jesus. In earliest childhood the voice of the Good Shepherd is heard—"Suffer little children to come unto Me"—and the Saviour reveals His love to tender lambs, and is delighted with their hosannahs. God often calls young men by His grace, and enables them to make the great choice; and instead of going away sorrowful, they gladly receive the word, and with full purpose of heart cleave unto the Lord, and become strong to overcome the wicked one. The hardening influ-

* A centurion under the Emperor Hadrian became in his old age a believer in Christ. He then retired from the Imperial Court, and lived in quietness for seven years. The following is the touching epitaph he wrote for himself: "Hic jacet Similis, cujus aetas multorum annorum fecit, ipse septum duntaxat vixit annos." (Here lies Similis, who reached an age of many years, and yet lived only seven years.)

ence of the world and of long habits, and the death-like security and unimpressionable ease which characterize man's later years, cannot resist the merciful power of the Holy Ghost when He touches heart and conscience, and reveals the Father's love and the Saviour's grace. And even after a long Christless life, and while the sun is already setting, the outstretched arms of Jesus are full of pity and compassion, and His word is heard, "To-day shalt thou be with Me in paradise."

Jesus is the lover of men, for He is the Son of God who loved the world. Jesus is the light, and when we come to Him, our true life and our everlasting day commence. Jesus is the door; and at any time, at any stage of our path, we may enter. Immediately we enter in our past guilt is forgiven, and a new beginning of thought, feeling, will, and energy is born within us. Then the path of life is before us. Seek not to walk on the narrow path before you have entered in at the strait gate; out of the old heart cannot come the new life, and in the strange country we cannot earn or procure the best robe, the ring of adoption, and the shoes in which we run the way of God's commandments. Christ is before us wherever we are: in our old sinful and unhappy condition, whether our past course was short or long, He is before us, the Door; the end of the times of ignorance—God's wisdom; the end of the works of the law—the righteousness of God; the end of our troubled and hardened conscience—perfect acceptance and peace; the end of our selfish and worldly life—sanctification. Only enter in, and the old things have passed away. Behold all things have become new.

If we have entered in, then let us work the works of Him that sent us while it is day. Great is the reward which, of His abundant grace, God will give us for all labour, suffering, patience; for every ministry of love to the brethren, to afflicted humanity; for all loyal testimony and service.

We may convert, even now, everything into a divine reward. The things which we are accustomed to view as full of sorrow, privation, and difficulty, may be turned into sources of joy, strength, and riches. If in affliction we learn faith, humility, patience, we obtain blessings which endure for ever. The trial, which seems to be fiery, burns only fetters of sin and worldliness; it takes nothing from our true self, but only adds health, strength, and beauty, which can never fade. Have we experienced the injustice, ingratitude, faithlessness, or hatred of men? they cannot truly injure us as long as we do the will of God; nay, they cannot help being our benefactors, enriching us with heavenly treasure, if we forgive their trespasses and, in communion with Jesus, do the Christlike work of loving them and praying for them. Let us learn from our Lord Jesus, to whom all He experienced on earth became only material and nourishment of His divine love-fire. When Pharisees murmured, He in reply uttered the most touching and tender parables of the divine joy in receiving sinners. When men crucified Him, His all-forgiving, all-enduring love shone forth only with greater brightness. Nothing can affect the purity, the kindliness, the generosity of the light; nothing can defile, dim, or extinguish the fire of love. One who had great sufferings, and for many long years, was able to say: "Our *light* affliction, which is but for a *moment*, worketh for us a far more exceeding and eternal weight of glory."* That which seems to work only injury; pain to the body, sadness to the soul, hindrance to our usefulness; in reality, and seen by faith, works for us our everlasting blessedness. Say no longer of your trials and hardships, of your losses and disappointments, of your sickness and infirmity: "All these things are against me;" but rather reckon them among the all things which work

---

* 2 Cor. iv. 17.

together for good unto you who love God. Our sufferings are our eternal ornaments; what we give away, our everlasting possession; our thorns, never-fading flowers.

In the false and garish light of the world, health and wealth, the honour which cometh from man, earthly wisdom and wit, prosperity and influence, are the only things which are seen to be bright and beautiful. But God looks upon the broken and contrite heart, the meek and the quiet spirit, faith and joy in His beloved Son, crucifixion of the flesh, and the fellowship of Christ's sufferings; these appear to Him beautiful, and are His delight. And it is in the school of suffering that we learn the wisdom which is from above; it is in the furnace of affliction that our faith is tried, that it may be found unto praise, and honour, and glory. If you feel "it is towards evening, and the day is far spent," only constrain Jesus to abide with you; and when He makes Himself known, when He enters the heart and holds there the supper with His downcast disciple, your youth, your glowing affections, your joyous hopefulness, will be renewed, and you will be able to say: "The Lord is risen again," and go on your way rejoicing.

"The night cometh." In the mouth of the Lord Jesus these words had a peculiar significance. The night which came to Jesus was the result of our sin, the fruit of our disobedience; it was the hour and power of darkness. His love to us was willing to enter even into this night. *Jesus died; believers only fall asleep.* Jesus was made sin for us; nay, He was made a curse, and entered into the agony of the three hours, when God hid from Him His countenance. Believers do not *see* death; for "the sting of death is sin; and the strength of sin is the law; but thanks be to God, which giveth us the victory." Let us therefore not be afraid of the night; let us work in Christ and for Christ while it is day. This is the solemnity, the unique importance of our life-day, that it stands in *immediate* connection with that day, when the Lord, the righteous Judge, will give the crown, the reward for labour, to all His disciples. The apostle Paul looked from the hour of his departure, when he finished his course, having kept the faith, to the appearing of our Lord. He looked past the intervening period. It has no relation to his ultimate reward. The night which comes to believers is rest, but rest in communion with Christ; it is sleep, but sleep in Jesus. They rest from their labours, waiting for the resurrection morning, when Christ shall appear, and they with Him.*

---

* John viii. 51; 1 Cor. xv. 55-57; 2 Tim. iv. 7, 8.

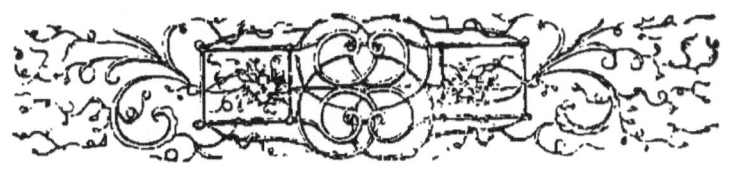

CHAPTER V.

From Morn to Eve: the Six Ages of Man.

"While it is day: the night cometh, when no man can work."
John ix. 4.

IT is the glory of man that he is utterly dependent on God. Apart from God human life is unintelligible and wretched. We are not able to understand ourselves. Our whole existence is a dark problem, bewildering and oppressive, until, beholding ourselves in the mirror of God, we say, in the full presence of the most High: " Thou, God, seest me." The only light which brings light and peace to us is the personal living God, the all-seeing and all-loving One, "in whom we live, and move, and have our being." "Know thyself" is the counsel of wisdom from the most ancient days. We do not know ourselves, and this ignorance is our misery; but this is our all-sufficient consolation, that, an enigma to ourselves, we are perfectly known of God.

In one of the most wonderful psalms of David (Psalm cxxxix) this thought is expressed with the singular power and impressiveness which characterise this portion of the inspired word. The psalmist realises God's omnipresence and omniscience as concentrated upon himself—" O Lord, Thou hast searched me, and known me. Thou knowest my downsitting and mine uprising, Thou understandest my thought afar off. Thou compassest my path and my lying down, and art acquainted with all my ways. For there is not a word in my tongue, but, lo, O Lord, Thou knowest it altogether. Thou hast beset me behind and before, and laid thine hand upon me." In this vivid sense of the depth as well as the breadth of God's omnipresence and omniscience David feels himself enclosed by the knowledge and presence of Him who is the infinite source and sovereign author of all created spirits. As God is the only One who has a perfect, all-comprehensive knowledge of our *present* ways and thoughts, and the inmost springs of our being, so it is He to whom were known the very beginnings of our existence, whose wisdom, power, and goodness were glorified in the mysterious and hidden commencement of our earthly life, and who determined beforehand our whole path. "For thou hast possessed my reins: Thou hast covered me in my mother's womb. I will praise Thee; for I am fearfully and wonderfully made;...and that my soul knoweth right well. My substance was not hid from Thee, when I was made in secret, and curiously wrought in the lowest parts of the earth. Thine eyes did see my substance, yet being unperfect; and in Thy book all my members were written, which in continuance were fashioned, when as yet there was none of them."

Such knowledge, he confesses, is too wonderful for him; it is so high he cannot attain unto it. But as it is high, so it is full of comfort. The omniscient eye, to which he is perfectly known and transparent, the omnipotent hand, which has formed him from his very origin, belong to Him who is love, and who leads us in the way everlasting.* It humbles us, but it also elevates us, that it is God who sent us into this world, who alone fixes the time when we are to depart, that all our times are in His hand, that all our springs are in Him. We are always as helpless and as dependent on Him as in the hour of our birth and the hour of our death; for He is God.

* Psalm cxxxix. 24.

We may think it a very common-place truth, and one of which we need scarcely to be reminded, "It is God that hath made us, and not we ourselves;"* and yet it is this simple but fundamental truth which by the grace of God's Spirit can alone give us the victory over the multiform enemy with which we have to contend, our self-will. Only when we remember that God is our sovereign Creator can we successfully resist the assertion of our self-will, our self-dependence, which is the root of all our sins, whether it manifest itself as pride, or gloomy discontent, or despondency, or the love of pleasure. And when we have learned to bow before the Lord as God, then out of this knowledge of the sovereignty of God our Creator, peace and consolation will flow into our hearts. Because we are the work of His hands, He will never forsake us, but perfect that which concerneth us; for His mercy endureth for ever. Because we know that He is God, that it is He who hath made us, and not we ourselves, we "serve the Lord with gladness, and come before His presence with singing . . . we are His people, and the sheep of His pasture."† He is near us, with us, in us. As our hearts lie open before Him, all our wants and sorrows, our difficulties and infirmities, our sins

† Psalm c. 3.   * Psalm c. 2, 3.

and failures appeal to His all-powerful love, and there is nothing in us which is not accessible to His mercy and might. "I am thine." This is the language of humility; it is the all-prevailing plea of the child of God, and the never-failing consolation in time of trouble and distress. We are the object of His electing love, the work of His almighty and allwise hands, the triumph of His redeeming grace. And ultimately we shall stand before Him, the perfect embodiment and fulfilment of His eternal thought and purpose, when we shall be conformed to the image of His Son, and glorified together with Christ shall, as the firstfruits of His creature, show forth His manifold wisdom and power.*

There is no period of our existence in which we are not precious in His sight, as there is none in which we are not utterly dependent on His goodness and care. We readily acknowledge the frailty and helplessness of infancy and of childhood; but we are equally, and in some respects growingly, dependent on God in our youth and manhood, in the evening hours of life, and in the last hours and moments of our earthly pilgrimage. The humble soul rejoices in this dependence, even as the all-generous God delights in being our shelter, our

* Rom. viii. 29; James i. 18.

strength, and our everlasting home. God, who is our only help, who is nearer to us than we are to ourselves, regards us ever with the deepest and most loving interest. No mother watches all the manifestations of the child's growth and development with more tender love; no gardener looks with kindlier care and delight on his flowers and plants from the very commencement of their existence, than God watches our infancy and childhood, our youth, and the years of our maturity and strength, and the days which, to the outward observer, seems days of declining life and of decay, but which to God are days of inward renewal and of hastening to the ultimate glory.

This thought is full of comfort. But we need this comfort; for not merely do we depend all the days of our life on divine power and goodness; we also depend on His forgiving, renewing, and sanctifying grace; because there is no age in which sin is not around and within us. We bring sin with us into the world. However we may explain the awful mystery, we cannot deny the fact that we are all born in sin, and that there is within us, from our very birth, the germ of that gigantic evil—enmity against God. In our infancy sin is quiescent, and it seems difficult to believe that in the tender and beautiful flower there is already the hateful germ. Yet before we are able to express our thoughts and feelings in words, our features and actions betray the motions of self-will, of impatience, of jealousy.* Childhood is comparatively pure and innocent; sin still slumbers, but still it is there. It shows itself in many grievous ways; foolishness is bound up in the heart of a child. Parents and teachers can see in the microcosm of the child's heart, as it manifests itself in the child's ways, much which justly excites their grave anxiety, and merits their true sorrow and displeasure. Childhood merges into youth, and then follow the earnest, sober, and laborious years of manhood, and the still more solemn and thoughtful years of old age. But though the form of sin changes, though the lust of the flesh, the lust of the eye, and the pride of life, the love of pleasure, ambition, avarice, may belong to various stages of our life, sin itself, in its God-opposed nature, remains the same—remains ever within us. And sin is a most fearful evil. Alas! we are so used to the thought and fact that sin is in us all the days of our life, that we do but rarely get a glimpse of its true character; that but rarely the sight of sin sends as it were an electric shock of pain and self-abhorrence through our souls.

* Augustine, *Confess. I.*

How used we are to have that fire burning within us, which is radically connected with the fire of hell and the everlasting depths. How little alarmed do we feel that sin is harboured by our souls; that loathsome leprosy, that corroding disease, that inexorable cancer, sin, which is regarded by the holy angels with unspeakable dismay and horror, which calls forth wrath in the bosom of infinite love, which is the source, and only source, of all misery both in this world and that which is to come. And to sin we get used! It causes us but rarely alarm; we shed but few tears over it; and when we discover it in our hearts, and in our lives, we feel but little and short-lived grief. Sin is in us all the days of our life. What would become of us if divine mercy was not with us from our birth to our death?

And as sin is within us, it is always around us. We are not like Jesus, whose heart was hermetically closed against all evil, so that the world and the temptations of Satan could not touch Him, or for a moment cause His will to vibrate in the God-opposed direction. Too readily do we inhale as fragrance the poisonous atmosphere; too easily do we allow the tempter to fill our imagination with his beautiful phantasmagoria, our reason with his sophistical dialectics, and our heart with doubt of

God's truth and God's love. From this inward defeat to outward transgression of God's commandment is but an easy step. Satan, the great adversary, one of whose stratagems is to make both world and church forget his existence, and become ignorant of his methods, is our tempter throughout life. Think of His cruelty, that he does not spare the tender child. He regards neither the beauty and frailty of childhood, nor the sweet prayers of a mother and the earnest affection of a father, nor the loving presence of the watchers, the holy angels, nor the special tenderness and guarding eye of the heavenly Father. Satan seeks to fan the sinful spark in the child's soul, and like a very wolf endeavours to destroy the little lambs. And think of Satan's perseverance and persistence. He despairs not of the dying saint; and when he is not able to tempt him with thoughts and imaginations of evil, he tries to divert him from God and Christ by the thought of self-righteousness and self-complacency.

Are we from infancy to death dependent on God's goodness and power on account of our weakness? how much more are we dependent on God's grace on account of our sinfulness and spiritual danger!

But God is rich in mercy towards all. He is

able to renew and to inhabit by His Spirit the infant. He sanctified John the Baptist even from the womb. Jesus can touch the little ones whom as yet He cannot teach; He can transplant them into the kingdom of God; He can make these tender yet sinful branches of the Adam-tree members of His mystical body. God is able to incline the hearts of young children to hear the Good Shepherd's voice, so that they may come unto Him, to be folded in His arms. In our youth, when temptation is strongest, God can constrain us by the love of Christ, and filled with humility and faith young men have the word of God abiding in them, and overcome the wicked one.* The grace of God can visit us in our manhood, when the world is too much with us, and we have settled down in the habit of a Christless existence. The grace of God which bringeth salvation hath appeared unto all men, from the babe to the man, who on the very threshold of the grave utters the petition, "Lord, remember Thou me!"

How full of comfort are these truths, when we think of the problem of life. Let me conclude these general remarks by reminding you again of the crowning consolation. Adam was sent into

* 1 John ii. 13, 14.

the world in the form of ripe and fully-developed manhood; but when the Son of God undertook and condescended to redeem mankind, He did "not abhor the virgin's womb." He went through human life in all its phases. He lived as an infant, a child, a youth, and through the years of mature manhood, to sanctify every age, and to be an example to all.* He has presented unto His Father, who in Him is also our Father, the whole of human life from its mysterious commencement to its termination in death, and throughout this life only that which is pleasing to the holy God; and if we believe in Jesus we are represented in Him, and every phase of our life, every part of our path, is consecrated by the perfection of the incarnate Son.

When we remember all these things we can look upon human life with thankfulness, with humble trust, nay, with adoring joy. Notwithstanding the many afflictions, trials, sorrows; the problems which we cannot solve in this valley, but which await their full solution in the bright hereafter; though there are many tears which even God does not wipe from our eyes until we are before His throne, yet can we thank God for our creation, yet can we rejoice that we belong to

* An oft-quoted remark of Irenaeus.

humanity; that unto us a child was born, a Son was given; that the Word was made flesh, and dwelt among us; that in our nature He glorified the Father; that in our exalted Lord dwelleth the fulness of the Godhead bodily. We rejoice that we belong to the many sons whom the Captain of our salvation is leading to glory; we rejoice that we are joint-heirs with Christ Jesus, and that throughout all ages we shall remember the wondrous story of His incarnation and birth, of His childhood and baptism, of His obedience and death on the cross—"the perfect life-day of the eternal Son."

I. INFANCY.

David often thinks of the helpless years of infancy; nay, of the hour of his birth, and how God was then the strength and help of his mother. He reminds himself of this in the dark days of affliction, sorrow, and trial. In that most solemn psalm which found its fulfilment in the cry of our Lord Jesus on the cross, David says: "But thou art He that took me out of the womb: thou didst make me be in safety when I was upon my mother's breasts." Is it not good for us also to remember the wonderful and spontaneous goodness of our God, before we even knew our helplessness, and were able to send a prayer or a sigh to His heavenly throne? His infinite love, self-moved, looked down upon us with compassion and tenderness. Let us think of it with gratitude, and derive from it hope and encouragement. However helpless and weak we may become again, the strong arms of everlasting love are ever ready to guard, nurse, and help that which is utterly feeble. He who was our help will be the same faithful Creator to the end. When we meet anyone who says to us, "You may not remember me, but I knew you when you were a little child; I was your father's and mother's friend; I have often played with you when you were yet in your mother's arms," does not our heart warm to him? and can we ever fear any evil from his hands? Such was the appeal of David to God, the God of his infancy, the God of his mother: "I am thy servant, the son of thy handmaid: thou hast loosed my bonds." And to this feeling God Himself appeals, when He encourages Isaac, by saying that He was the God of his father; and Jacob, that He was the God of his father Isaac and of his father Abraham.*

But infancy is not merely the object of God's tender and loving care, it is also the object of His marvellous wisdom and power. We do not re-

* Ps. xxii. 9, cxvi. 16; Gen. xxv. 3, xxviii. 13.

member the days of our infancy, and the life which our immortal spirit lived then is altogether hidden from us. If some angel were to tell us what then passed within the sanctuary of our soul, we should perhaps understand it as little as our memory can recall anything belonging to the dawn of our life. Well may we believe the apostle's declaration, "It doth not yet appear what we shall be," when our infancy is so incomprehensible to us.* Parents also who watched us with intense and constant affection could only observe what is outward; but their eye could not penetrate into the inner life. But God beheld and knew the life within. When the daughter of Pharaoh opened the little ark of bulrushes, and beheld that tiny babe, whose tear-filled eyes were scarcely able to bear the light of day, and whose feeble arms appealed for help, all the powers of mind which afterwards characterised Moses, the man of God, were already in existence in that tender child. All those mental gifts, all those wonderful powers of the soul and spirit, were already there which manifested themselves afterwards in the man who brought Israel out of Egypt, and through whom God gave His law and covenant to His people. There was nothing added afterwards, there was only development.

* J. H. Newman.

Before the power of reasoning manifests itself reason exists; before volition shows itself there is the will. And, as we experience subsequently, God Himself has implanted within us eternal mother-ideas—primary, axiomatic, fundamental—which cannot and need not be proved, from which we constantly start, and into which we constantly recede, to bring out what we need and seek. The image of God, in which we are created, is stamped on our soul from its commencement. God sees in the infant all that the germ contains.

Still more wonderful is it to think that God is able to enter into this apparently inaccessible shrine, and that the Holy Ghost can influence the infant spirit. What that direct sanctifying influence is we cannot imagine, as we know of scarcely any other influence except that of teaching and persuasion, indirect influence through the avenues of thought and affection. The eternal life of which infants partake who are called from earth to the immediate beholding of God's countenance must to some extent have commenced here on earth. Hidden to the eye of man, and inaccessible even to his thought, the Spirit of God has brought the light and life of God, has brought Christ to the infant soul.

II. CHILDHOOD.

The infant develops into the child. Self-consciousness dawns; the thoughtful and self-conscious spirit begins to manifest itself in utterance, the child speaks. Language, that rubicon which no lower animal ever crosses, reveals the dignity of one only a little lower than the angels.* We admire the stupendous works of creation. The glorious heavens, the work of God's fingers; the sun, the moon, and the stars, which He has ordained; all the marvellous works of God—as beautiful to-day as they were the moment of their birth. We see God's skill and power in the majestic mountains and rocks, and still more in the plant-world, the flowers and trees; but what is this all, compared with the marvel of a babe's first utterance? Out of the mouth of babes God has ordained praise for Himself. Man is the centre of God's creation, the link between spirit and nature; he is member of a race, and partakes thus of the life of nature, is subject to its laws, and apparently like the lower animals; and he belongs also to the spirit world, he possesses an individual spirit, he is created in God's image, and to find life in communion

* Psalm viii.

with the Father in heaven. It is for this reason that we feel God so near, when we watch the first dawn of self-conscious life in the child; that with reverence and in joy we welcome the little brother-pilgrim to our God-given inheritance—eternity.

There is in all of us a feeling of reverence and affection towards the days of our childhood. But it is only Christ who has taught mankind to understand its true meaning and exquisite beauty; even as He only restores to us the childlike spirit, and will ultimately grant us the fulfilment and perfection of which childhood is an emblem and prophetic intimation. Antiquity did not truly appreciate childhood. When man had departed from the Father's house, and in that spirit of self-dependence* which is the root of all sin and misery had gone into a far country, he lost the true, profound, and exquisitely sweet meaning of child-life. Not knowing the true nature of humility, and complete yet joyous subordination to another will, childhood was viewed chiefly as a very imperfect phase which was necessary in order to reach manly strength and wisdom; but which in itself had no substantial value, which formed no ever-abiding treasure, and which contained no emblem and lesson for our

* αὐτάρκεια.

whole life. It was Jesus who taught us what is meant by God in children. Jesus was the first who set a child in the midst of the disciples as an emblem of the heavenly, spiritual mind. Once the great thought was uttered by the Holy Child of God, the Wisdom from above, the conscience and heart instinctively received it as a true and beautiful revelation. Now we know what is meant by "childlike."*

In bringing before us the mind of little children, our Lord avails Himself of a principle in our nature which makes us regard our childhood with tenderness, and at the same time He makes it easy for most of us to observe the characteristics of the true believer. The simplicity, the unassuming guilelessness, the unconscious humility, the peaceful contentedness with the present, the sweet docility, which does not think it strange, or irksome, or degrading, to be continually instructed, moulded, corrected, but receives counsel and rebuke with an open and loving heart—who has not noticed these lovely features of childhood? The constant influence of a superior mind, instead of raising a wall of separation, or infusing a spirit of bitterness, becomes rather a link of sweet and tender affection, which subsequent years cannot

* Matt. xviii. 3; xix. 14.

break or enfeeble. From a child learn the spirit of discipleship.

A child is earnest. With all its playfulness childhood is characterized by deep solemnity. Children are ready to believe things unseen, and eager to hear about God. They listen with awe and reverence; they find it easy to believe in prayer; they look for immediate obedience to God's precepts.

Again, a child is frank and confiding. It is calm, and free from care and anxiety; joyous in thanksgiving; humble without effort; ready to treat all human beings with affection, resting in the known love of parents and teachers.

Childhood has a peculiarly spiritual and real character. As yet time and strength are not occupied with the distractions of earthly work and worldly influences. The will also, with its disturbing motions, seeking to assert self as a centre, is as yet comparatively quiet, and mind and heart are free and open to receive impressions and to respond to truth and love. At leisure from himself the child is willing to learn, to see, and to hear. Everything in childhood has the character of education; all that is done, and all that happens, goes to the formation of the future or inner man. Parents and teachers are continually directing, rebuking, moulding; the whole life is under rule, guidance, and restraint. But the one constant object is the *child himself*, his character, his present and future welfare. The whole day, with its lessons and recreations, is devoted to the true and real interests of the child. The child is treated with true love, with true humanity, not as a means to an end, but as the sacred and precious object itself. We shrink from the utterance of a single word, or even from manifesting a look, that could disturb the purity of the child, or in any way injure its spiritual growth. And so children lead a most real and true life before God; sheltered from the artificial and unprofitable world of unrealities, as well as from the mechanical toil and hollow ambition with which we have subsequently to contend. Hence among our most beautiful and fragrant recollections we treasure in after-life the solemn, real, and peaceful school-days of our childhood.

God, in holy Scripture, gives a very important place to children. When He brings His people out of Egypt He remembers especially the little ones. In all the laws and statutes which He gave through His servant Moses God seems to have almost more regard to the children than to the grown-up people. With great frequency and earnestness He exhorts the fathers to teach His precepts and commandments to their children, and by daily conversation to impress them on the receptive minds of their little ones. In ordaining the beautiful festivals God pictures the family circle, and the thoughtful little faces, with their eager questions in that spirit of virgin-wonder which God has given to childhood, and provides the answers which are to be remembered and repeated from generation to generation. When God entered into covenant with Abraham He remembered the whole household. When the law was read before all people, God commanded the children also to be gathered, and makes special mention of the children of the stranger "within thy gates ... and that their children, which have not known anything, may hear, and learn to fear the Lord your God."* Thus Joshua read the law before all the congregation, "with the women, and all the little ones."† When Jesus sends His messengers, He sends them not merely to the individual, but to the whole family. "Peace be to this house," is their salutation, and their message: "Believe in the Lord Jesus Christ, and thou shalt be saved, and thy house."‡

God, who loves children, holds constant intercourse with children. He influences their minds

---

* Deut. xxxi. 12, 13.   † Josh. viii. 35.
‡ Luke x. 5 ; Acts xvi. 31.

and hearts continually, even as He watches over their bodies. Look back on your own childhood. Examine the deepest, the most fundamental impressions which you have received, the profound thoughts and feelings to which you are always brought back. Holiness, love, eternity, the Father in heaven — these great thoughts, too great, vast, and deep for words, live in you now as they first awoke within your heart in your childhood. You can almost recall the child's feeling, as these thoughts were first realised and uttered. Do we not receive in childhood the true idea of repentance, of the sweetness of repentance, when, after the hard and miserable hours of self-will, disobedience, and isolation, the child, with mingled sorrow and hope, self-condemnation and yearning affection, returns to the father, and is humbled and elevated by his forgiving and restoring love? Did not God then teach us in parable that it is a bitter thing to depart from Him, but truly a sweet and blessed thing to return unto the Lord our God; for unto Him belong mercies and forgivenesses?

But the Lord often leads children, not merely into the sanctuary, but into the holy of holies. The child's heart, which has often been filled with solemn reverence, with joyous gratitude, with trembling adoration, with tender love, may yet, like little Samuel, surrounded with sacred emblems and prepared by divine teaching, never have heard the voice of God, the direct, personal, saving call of the Lord. But at last the hour approaches; the Holy Ghost enlightens the mind and touches the heart; the presence of God is felt; the love of Jesus, who died for the flock, brings true peace, and another lamb is within the fold of the Good Shepherd. The divine Friend of children on His heavenly throne delights in their Hosannah. He is able to feed the lambs, to reveal Himself unto their hearts, to teach them from their earliest days heavenly wisdom. And many a long life-day of service and testimony has commenced in the very first hours of morning.

The impression that children who are brought early to the knowledge and love of Christ are soon called away from this life, is not founded on extensive observation. From the Scripture biographies, and from Church history, it appears that many who received the grace of God in childhood, served God and laboured for Christ during a long life, and thus gave full evidence of the reality of their early conversion. We must not doubt the genuineness of a child's Christian faith; but we must bear in mind that as the child develops it needs instruction, guidance, warning. The central knowledge and love of God need to be deepened, as mental power develops and the whole circle of life enlarges. There are many spiritual dangers and diseases to be guarded against; above all, there is much need of constant, wholesome, and varied spiritual nourishment.

III. YOUTH.

Childhood merges into youth. Even though we have as children come to know God, youth is the age when we must make again, and with fuller knowledge and purpose, the great choice.* It is a crisis. Our mental and physical powers develop; our own individuality manifests itself, with its peculiar gifts and aspirations; the world opens before us in all its manifold beauty, and with its various calls to exertion. We ask ourselves, "What is to be my life, my task, my happiness?" We seek also the object on which to centre our affection.

All nations have recognised the great importance of youth. They have regarded youth as the most solemn and momentous age of life. The story of Hercules and the choice between pleasure

---

* Compare my "Conversion, Illustrated by Examples recorded in the Bible." Timothy, chap. vi.

and virtue, expresses the sentiment of all mankind. But we possess more than earthly wisdom and experience; to us is given God's own word, that it may be a light on our path. Throughout Scripture there is special instruction for the young. In the Proverbs of Solomon, the unsurpassed guide-book of youth, the simplicity of childhood, fearing and loving the Lord, is beheld developing into wisdom, prudence, understanding, in the manifold temptations and relationships of life.

The young need guidance; for in the multitude of new thoughts, impulses, and prospects, they become confused and perplexed. God invites us to ask Him to be the guide of our youth. They need not merely the guidance of wisdom, but the constraining influence of divine love; for sin and the world possess peculiar power and fascination for the young. The Lord is able not only to teach but to touch the heart, and to guide into the way everlasting.

The second thing specially needed in youth is a purifying and cleansing power. Sin, which slumbered in infancy, which was quiescent in childhood, now asserts itself with great strength; for the simple reason that now the self-consciousness is intense, and sin in its root is the assertion of *self*, in whatever form, be it in pride, ambition, the love of pleasure, or any other of the myriad manifestations it assumes. "Wherewithal shall a young man *cleanse* his way?" is the question of the psalmist. And the answer points to the word of life—"By taking heed thereto according to thy word."* The conscience must be first purified and set free by faith in Christ, our atonement; and the heart must be continually influenced by faith, by looking unto Jesus, by beholding the things unseen and eternal.

Youth longs above all for love. God has given to us earthly love, that we may be drawn by it to Himself, and to that only one and indivisible divine love. In the love of the creature, apart from God, we can never find rest for our heart.

> "Something every heart is loving;
> If not Jesus, none can rest."

The only object of the soul's love is God Himself. Youth finds happiness only then when it can appropriate the words of the psalmist: "With my heart do I love thee, O Lord, my strength."† The disciple whom Jesus loves rests on the bosom of eternal love and blessedness. Our hearts are made for God, and are never at peace till we come to Him.

Youth stands on the cross-road between pleasant

---

* Psalm cxix. 9. † Psalm xviii., original.

vice and austere virtue, between the smooth road and the thorny path; but does it possess a mind free and unbiassed, a heart unoccupied and innocent, that it will be able to make a real *choice?* Blessed by God we place before youth not a choice merely, but a magnet. The voice that says, "Give me, My son, thy heart," speaks with divine authority, with constraining love, with will-renewing power. It is the voice of Him who formed the heart, who alone can satisfy it, who alone can mould it. And the magnet which God has appointed to draw our hearts is His own Son; and that by which His own Son draws hearts to Himself is by His dying love. "And I, when I am lifted up, will draw all men unto Me." Is it strange that it is so? that the love of Christ, dying for the ungodly, should decide the choice, should break the will, and melt the heart? Of all the decisions described in Scripture that of Moses seems to me the most touching. There came to Moses, as to each one of us, the time when he had to choose his path. The choice was between God and the world; between the service of Jehovah and the heathen court, with its idolatry and its honours and pleasures. He was the only Hebrew who was free to keep aloof from the despised nation, the only one in whom it required a voluntary sacrifice to be numbered among the persecuted race. And in this choice between worldly ambition and happiness, and suffering and shame, what was it that gave the decision? It was nothing else but the reproach of Christ. It was the bleeding Lamb of God. Beholding the cause of God's truth and people suffering in a world of idolatry, sin, and cruelty, Moses esteemed the reproach of Christ greater riches than the treasures of Egypt. And thus is it with every one who is truly brought to God. It is true he sees the recompence of the reward, the everlasting blessedness, the unfading crown. But that which attracts him immediately and with most direct power is Christ crucified. He says, "God forbid that I should glory, save in the cross of our Lord Jesus Christ, by whom the world is crucified unto me, and I unto the world." He thanks God who has counted him worthy to be identified with the poor and afflicted people of the Son of God.

Blessed are the young who, beholding Christ crucified, despised and rejected of men, do not go away sorrowful, but gladly obey His call to take up the cross, to follow Him in humility, and to walk in the narrow way. The fellowship of Christ's sufferings will bring with it peace and joy such as the world cannot know, and while they are delivered from this present evil age, they possess the dignity of the citizens of heaven.

It has been remarked, that as in the two youthful figures, Achilles and Alexander, the one standing at the entrance, the other at the end of Grecian history, is mirrored the nature and life of the Hellenic people; so we behold at the commencement and at the end of the history of the Jewish theocracy two young men, in whom the spirit of the true Israelite is manifested with peculiar power and attractiveness—Joseph in Egypt, and Daniel in Babylon. Both passed through severe afflictions, trial, and temptation in tender youth; both were witnesses for the true God, and representatives of the chosen race at heathen courts; both were blameless in their pure walk, and by their elevated character and irreproachable conduct commended and adorned the doctrine of the gospel; both were endowed with wonderful insight and wisdom, and exemplified the prophetic character of Israel, the messengers of the divine, heaven-sent interpretation of the dreams and problems which the most renowned sages of heathenism could not understand. What illustrations do these two young men afford of integrity, single-heartedness, purity; of self-restraint and courage; of strength and of meekness; of high purpose, lofty intellect, and of childlike humility. Such and other noble and precious qualities are seen in them, and all proceeding from one centre—they walked with God. This is the explanation of their character and life. Godliness is their distinguishing feature. Joseph feared God from his childhood; the ungodly ways of his brothers grieved him, and the tender boy was attracted with peculiar power by his aged father, who honoured Jehovah. Zeal for the honour and righteousness of the chosen family filled his young heart. What many years after he said of himself—"I fear God"—was his motto from the very commencement. A deep and constant sense of the presence of the holy and loving Covenant-God characterises him from his youth. When tempted by sin, he thinks of God, and gains the victory. The thought of God enables him to bear patiently his imprisonment, and to fulfil his duties cheerfully and kindly. The thought of God keeps from him pride and self-trust, and invests his bearing before Pharaoh with dignified and beautiful humility. He remembered God at all times, and, as Stephen says in his last address, "God was with him."

The same godliness we see in Daniel. His faith in God was strong. Though Jerusalem was destroyed, and the chosen people were led into captivity, he believed in God and trusted in His word. No bitter disappointment and gloomy doubt weakened his joyous loyalty to Jehovah and His commandments. He had to exchange the dignity of a prince with a subordinate position. Tempted to conformity with the world, he purposed in his heart not to defile himself by transgressing the law of Moses. And while he thus retained the spirit of Jerusalem at Babylon's court, his decision and strength of character were combined with such sweetness and winning ingenuousness, that God brought him into favour and tender love with the prince of eunuchs. Add to this, that in all matters of wisdom and understanding he excelled all the magicians and astrologers of the realm. But although possessed of a lofty intellect, and of a mind profound and speculative, he was not led astray by philosophy, falsely so called, or beguiled from the simplicity of revealed truth. The wisdom of earth did not weaken or alter his faith in the God in heaven "who revealeth secrets." Such were Joseph and Daniel; they lived long and eventful lives, and their "old age was as their youth."*

But among the young men mentioned in Scrip-

* Deuteronomy xxxiii. 25 (Vulgate and Luther).

ture there is perhaps none who combines so many noble qualities as David. In secret, when no human eye was near, on the plains of Bethlehem the son of Jesse meditated on the sacred narratives which he had heard and read from his childhood, till faith in the God of Abraham, Isaac, and Jacob became the animating principle of his life and the strength of his soul. This faith was the victory which overcame the bear and the lion; and the presence of God became his shield and his sword. Throughout life God was his refuge and strength. The kindliness and tender affection which he felt to his flock remained ever in his heart, and in his old age he still feels towards his people as his poor sheep, whose sufferings are more than he can bear.

The contemplation of nature and the knowledge and love of the God of Israel filled his soul with melody; and of David in his youth we read that he played on his harp, even as we read of David at the end of his life, and as ever since he is remembered among God's people, "the anointed of the God of Jacob, and the sweet psalmist of Israel." (2 Samuel xxiii. 1.) Such heart-faith, tenderness, poetic inspiration, and spirit of melody we find in him, combined with valour, heroic courage, and prudence. The enthusiastic applause of Israel did not elate him; and the position which the anointing of Samuel gave him did not disturb his quiet, patient, and modest bearing. He was noble and generous in his conduct towards Saul. How patient was he when the fulfilment of the promise was delayed, when instead of the throne he had constant danger and hardship, when his master, who had at one time put all that he had into his hand, sought his life. All these long years he "mastered his heart; he was still;" he kept his hands clean, and his lips guileless; he was loyal throughout. Whence this elevation of character and sustained nobility? As David himself tells us in his Psalms, it was by faith, by his constant communion with God, by his seeking counsel from the Lord, and delighting himself in God as his God. He lifted up his soul to God at all times, and thus he was able to add to his many great virtues an overflowing thankfulness, and a triumphant joy in the God of his salvation. How difficult is it for us, when in safety and comfort, to say what David said in times of keenest suffering and greatest danger: "The Lord is my rock, and my fortress, and my deliverer, my God, my strength, in whom I will trust." And again, "I will bless the Lord at all times; His praise shall continually be in my mouth."

Youth, in all its peculiar beauty and strength,

has never found such an exponent as David—a brighter specimen of youthful idealism, poetic elevation, intuitive insight, chivalry, self-restraint, simplicity and unconsciousness, meekness and high-toned generosity. The hidden source of David's greatness was his faith in God. "Thou hast taught me from my youth," was his confession in his old age. His delight was in the law of the Lord, and he meditated on it day and night. It was the beauty of God that shone upon him.

III. MANHOOD.

God plants us in families. Marriage, instituted in Paradise, and anew consecrated and irradiated with typical glory at the feast of Cana, brings before us the great mystery of Christ and the Church. God blesses us with earthly love and communion; He gladdens our hearts and disciplines our souls by the sympathy and companionship of one united with us wholly and for life, in joy and sorrow, in work and rest, in all the various experiences of our pilgrimage. God puts upon us the dignity of fatherhood and of motherhood, places part of His own crown upon our heads, and anoints us prophets, priests, and kings in our homes. The great Lord of the harvest assigns to us our work, and gives us time and opportunity to develop our energies and to exercise the gifts entrusted to our stewardship. He sends the sunshine of prosperity. He chastens us also with affliction. He deals with us in His wisdom and love. Life becomes fuller and broader, and we attain greater strength and skill.

But what is the object of our life? Why does God not transplant us at once into the higher sanctuary? We are to be His witnesses; we are to glorify Him; we are also to attain to spiritual manhood and maturity; and lastly, we are to exert the power of Christian influence on those around us. It is just at this period of our life that our danger is to sink into spiritual languor and routine. We are apt to forget that, while not slothful in business, we must also be fervent in spirit. Our intellectual and social life expands, our interests multiply, our activities increase; but as the streams become more numerous is the fountain kept pure and strong? We read of one in Scripture who is indeed a model for men in the zenith of strength and usefulness. Daniel was the greatest man, after the king, in one of the most powerful empires which the world has ever seen. Out of one hundred and twenty men who were chosen to be rulers, three were elected "presidents."

Of these three Daniel was the first. Nay, the king would willingly have made him first in the whole monarchy, so wonderful was Daniel's wisdom, influence, and dignity. What a burden must have weighed incessantly upon his mind! The conflicting interests of many nationalities, the complex machinery of a state so vast and important, must have been a heavy burden of responsibility, and the object of ceaseless activity and toil. Although he was a foreigner, and his religion despised in the land and at the court, although he had no friends, and many envious and jealous detractors, yet all had to acknowledge that there was an excellent spirit in him.* What did they mean by an excellent spirit? Not the deep feelings of devotion, the inner principle of godliness, the enlightened views of Scripture truth. All this was a region unknown to them. But what they could see, and could not fail to observe, was what Jesus calls his "good works"—his integrity, his honour, his diligence, his loyalty, his justice, his candour, his kindliness, his benevolence, his wisdom, his patience, his self-control. What a man is brought before us here! Not a recluse, not a contemplative disciple, to whom has been granted the quiet life of solitude and prayer, but a

* Daniel vi. 3, 4.

man foremost in all the difficult problems of the state, overwhelmed with labour and responsibility, watched by all, and surrounded by perplexities and temptations. Yet the testimony of all is, that there is an excellent spirit in him. Look now at the source of his goodness and greatness. Look at the rock on which the beautiful building is reared. Look at the unseen fire which daily renews the bright flame. Daniel was a man of prayer. He made time for reading the Scripture, and for offering supplications unto God. Three times a day he felt it necessary, he felt it delightful, to retire from work unto direct communion with the Father in heaven. We read of John, the beloved disciple, that he leaned on the bosom of Jesus. But John was pre-eminently called to the contemplative life. We may think that our worldly and varied employments do not permit us to regard him as our model. But is it not as true of Daniel, the statesman, as it is of John, that he was the disciple whom Jehovah loved, and who leaned on Jehovah's arm?

The development of our spiritual and our natural life ought in some respects to coincide. The spiritual man, like every living organism, has his growth and development. The new man is *born* of incorruptible seed and by the word of truth. His life is perfect at his birth, and subsequently nothing can be added to it. But he needs growth; gifts and powers have to be developed and exercised. This is not merely an organic process, but also a spiritual life; it involves our labour and diligence, it employs our will and affections, and it is connected with our ultimate character and reward.

The apostle Paul speaks thus of two stages of the Christian life—the childish and the manly. The apostle John mentions also young men, and notices their strength and their victory over the wicked one.* It is evident that the fundamental characteristics of the children of God remain the same throughout; nay, that it is desirable to retain the peculiar characteristics of each age in that which succeeds it. But growth is an indispensable condition of health, and the Christian is to become "perfect;" that is, mature; to remain a child in malice, in understanding to become a man. The simplicity, the receptive joy, the first love of Christian childhood, can only remain true and genuine if we advance in knowledge, in the exercise of our gifts, in the active use of the grace bestowed on us. We must as Christians also pass from childhood and its peaceful schoolroom into the rough, laborious, and earnest school of life;

* 2 Cor. iii.; Heb. v. 12-14; 1 John ii. 12-14.

faith must be tested; love must be exercised; and the various sides of the Christian character must find their development. As youth in the natural life is a transition period—restless, full of new energies, as yet inharmonious, and seeking their ruler; full of zeal, which needs discipline; of self-reliance, which needs chastening; on the other side, ideal, generous, full of courage and devotion—so we have also in the spiritual life a period when we are strong, enterprising, ardent; when, like Peter, we promise never to deny the Master; when we gird ourselves, and go where it seems good to us. Yet may we at this stage be permitted to do some valiant things. God may honour our loyalty, our courage, our overflowing zeal and love to the souls of men. But there is the stage of manhood. There are some Christians who are men in knowledge of God and of His revelation, in experience of prayer, in humility and self-distrust, in patience, and in self-denying love. They are men also in this respect, that they have by prayer and practice so appropriated the gifts of God bestowed on them individually that their Christian character has been formed. Such Christians have power to teach, to influence, and to mould others. They are fathers, and in the gospel they beget children; they are spiritual, not easily shaken or moved, but possessing discernment, and able to endure temptation.*

Now when we have reached natural, we ought also to have attained to spiritual manhood; to a fuller knowledge and confirmed conviction of divine truth; to deeper insight into our own hearts, and to a more sustained trust in Christ; to greater skill in our conflict with sin and against the devices (methods) of the adversary; to greater fruitfulness in good works, and to more patient and helpful love towards our fellow-Christians and all men.

Christian maturity shows itself in *knowledge*. We are to be men in understanding. The apostolic prayer is, that believers may be filled with the spirit of wisdom and revelation in the knowledge of God. We are to "go on unto perfection." We have received the unction from above, from the Holy One, and therefore possess the power to know all things.† It is through the truth that the Father sanctifies us. Growth in the knowledge of Jesus Christ is the necessary manifestation of life. This knowledge increases not merely in compass, but in depth; it assumes the character of intense

---

* 1 Cor. xii. 8-10, iv. 15; Philemon 10; Heb. v. 14.

† 1 John ii. 20; Eph. i. 17; Col. i. 9; 1 Cor. xiv. 20; Heb. vi. 1.

conviction. In this respect mature Christians form a strong contrast to a peculiarity of our present age. A keen observer thus describes this feature of our day: "A weak generation feels it pleasant to be waved to and fro by every wind of doctrine; a childish and effeminate race deems it an advantage to have no fixed conviction, and would find it tiresome to continue with life-long loyalty in the one truth, and to find peace in the one thought." It is constant change—the intellectual activity and excitement in the search after truth, and not truth itself—which is their great object. Hence words, brilliant and subtle dialectics, negative doubts, and attacks on old opinions afford the nutriment of many minds. This tendency affects even Christians; but God has revealed to us by His Spirit Himself and the spiritual realities of His heavenly kingdom. We know the things freely given to us of God.* Jesus is the Truth. And the Spirit, whom we have received, leads us into the whole truth, according to the Saviour's promise. It does not become the Christian, with Christ his light, with the Holy Ghost his teacher, with Scripture his manual, to speak as the children of the age, who possess opinions, but not truth; who, seeking to establish a wisdom of their own, have

* 1 Cor. ii. 12.

not submitted themselves to the wisdom of God. But to be established in the truth is the characteristic of Christian manhood, the result of diligent, earnest, and conscientious study of God's word.

Connected with this knowledge and inward conviction is liberty and independence, in growing dependence on the one Master, and in the deepened sense of our responsibility to Him. The full-grown Christian is thankful to all brethren, teachers, ministries; but he is very jealous not to be moulded and influenced except by God's Spirit. He dreads superficial thoughts and words. He is on his guard against the tyranny of fashion, of majorities, of success, even in the Christian world. He strives against the love of praise, and studies to walk with God, to live always in secret, and to speak and act out of faith.*

Christian maturity has a deep experience of Christ's death and resurrection. All true conversion has this experience in germ. Our old man has been crucified with Christ; resurrection-life has been given to us by the risen Saviour; but we know, we feel, we experience it with greater distinctness, with keener self-condemnation, and with fuller joy. Our growth is, as it were, a

* Matt. xxiii. 8; 1 Cor. vii. 23.

growth out of and away from the old man: we have no confidence in the flesh, but a firmer reliance on Christ, more assured joy and more active and resolute drawing on the inexhaustible resources in Him.

More *active drawing* on the resources in Christ; for Christian maturity is earnestly occupied with the task, the work, the opportunity given by Christ. Christ is our life and strength, in order that we may follow Him as true disciples—that we may work for Him in His vineyard. Christ is our righteousness above; but it is also written, " He that doeth righteousness is righteous." Christ is our best robe; but it is also written, that we must put off the old man, and put on the Lord Jesus.* The Christian is a learner, and all learners must use diligence; they must practise, they must submit to discipline, they must not be discouraged by failure, they must not yield to sloth and despondency. As the Christian grows into Christ he regards the work in his own heart and life the most important. He takes heed first to himself, and then to teaching. He realises that the first object is to save himself, and that only then he can think of saving and helping others.† As the

---

* 1 John iii. 7 ; Eph. iv. 24 ; Rom. xiii. 14.
† 1 Tim. iv. 16; Matt. vii. 5.

self-righteous are anxious and jealous to realise their standard, so the Christ-righteous are anxious and energetic to work the works of Christ, and to walk even as Christ walked. And here they experience, that as all things come from the heart, so all things return to the heart. They therefore take heed to their words and acts, lest the heart be defiled and disturbed. They learn faithfulness in earthly things, that spiritual and true treasures may be entrusted to them. Christian maturity expresses itself in a greater importance attached to the cultivation of our own garden; to the secret life of prayer, meditation, and self-restraint; to the faithful performance of duty; to the lowly obedience of the well-known commandments and precepts, and that for the very reason that the Christian's great object is to win Christ, and to be found in Him; to fulfil the Master's command, "Occupy till I come;" and to be useful to the Church and world.

The Christian thus "gives all diligence, to add to his faith virtue; and to virtue knowledge; and to knowledge temperance; and to temperance patience; and to patience godliness; and to godliness brotherly kindness; and to brotherly kindness charity;" and thus he is "neither barren nor unfruitful in the knowledge of our Lord Jesus

Christ."* For as these things are the fruit of the Spirit, and can only appear where there is the saving knowledge of the Lord, so they all confirm and deepen us in our inward spiritual communion with Christ. The man of God is always on his guard against a false quietism. He rests in the grace of God, but in order to live and work by it; he relies on the promises, but in order to test them in the duties and trials of life; he beholds with open face the glory of the Lord, that he may be transformed by His Spirit. The word of God thus becomes really his;† it fulfils its purpose, "that the man of God may be perfect, throughly furnished unto all good works."

There is at the same time the definite and resolute conflict with his sin. We are to lay aside all guile and malice, all uncharitableness and evil speakings and hypocrisies; to put away the old leaven, to lay apart all filthiness and superfluity of naughtiness. The epistles speak as categorically as the law, both in positive and negative commandments; and yet they are not legal, for they address the spiritual man, in whom God works to will and to do. It is necessary that he be so

---

* 2 Peter i. 5-8.

† "A man's property consists of good things, which he can *skilfully use.*"—RUSKIN.

addressed, and it is part of the Christian's more mature wisdom that he acknowledges the necessity and feels thankful for the exhortations.

Yet with all this activity the Christian does not make his sanctification the object of his contemplation. His rest is always in Jesus. He does not look to Jesus as He is reflected in his heart, character, and walk, but to Jesus Himself, the Lamb that was slain for us, our righteousness and advocate, our life and glory. If we do not rest in Jesus, in whom the Father sees us perfect, we rest in our own attainment of godliness and in the testimony of our own conscience. He that sets up his sanctification to look at, as an old author remarks, sets up the greatest idol, which will ultimately strengthen his fears and doubts, though at first it may soothe his feelings and please his imagination.* Experience teaches us the subtle danger of this temptation; and we look again simply and exclusively unto Christ. For in this activity, in this striving according to His working, which worketh in us mightily, there is not merely rest in Jesus, but amidst our conscious failures and the constant presence of sin we are upheld by *Hope* of our ultimate deliverance, of our complete redemption, of our future glory. We

* Compare my "Hebrews," vol. i. p. 160, &c.

are saved by hope, and not in the complacent beholding of our progress.

The bond of perfectness is love. Walk in love is the most comprehensive rule. Love is the fulfilling of the law. Love never ceaseth, and will be our eternal blessedness when our knowledge and strength will be perfect. In proportion as we love, we have made progress in the school and service of Christ. The spiritual men, who are no longer babes, feel the pre-eminence of love, and endeavour to hold fast the unity of the Spirit in the bond of peace.*

Our education is in the hands of our heavenly Father. His great object is the health and prosperity of our inner man; His end is to conform us to the image of Christ, to bring us to glory. Affliction is one of the most important methods in the divine school. We must, according to a necessary law, through much tribulation enter into the kingdom of God. All children are partakers of chastisement. Many and manifold are our afflictions and trials. God knows and reaches the hidden point where we are most sensitive; He lays bare to us our subtle idolatry; He confounds our secret pride and self-confidence; He removes from our eye goals and rewards of our own choice;

* 1 Cor. iii. 3; xiii.; Eph. iv. 3.

He tries our faith by sufferings and disappointments for which we can discover no cause or object. We learn patience, we become inwardly humble, and wonder how we have had so little of the meekness and long-suffering of Christ towards others.

In the school of affliction as we grow in grace so the consciousness of our weakness and of our sinfulness increases, and we descend into the valley of humiliation. And yet we do not give up hope; nay, we become strong in faith, and our peace is more fully established; for we learn now to separate between flesh and spirit, between nature and grace, and to look unto the Lord, our never-failing Saviour. We see now clearly that the fountain of our life is not within us, not even in the new man, but that it is above, in Christ; that we are poor, nay, entirely empty, and not able to meet even the smallest demand on our patience, love, or faith; but that our Lord in heaven is rich, and that we can take out of His fulness and grace for grace. Christ, what He is and what He possesses: this is our portion; this is the substratum of our existence, and the ever-ready supply to meet all our circumstances. We are complete in Him; that is, though all below is empty, dry, and exhausted, in Him is the all-sufficient grace, the abundant and blessed fountain; *it is in Him, but it is for us.*

Above all, in their deepest trials and sufferings God's children—and the most experienced most—cling to the faithful saying, worthy of all acceptation, to Christ Jesus, who came into the world to save sinners. When all within is cold and parched up, when the feeling of our sin and unworthiness oppresses our hearts, when, like Job, we behold anew that we are vile, then Christ, crucified for our offences and raised for our justification, is our only—but our all-sufficient—stay and trust.

In the formation of the Christian character there is thus much labour, conflict, and sorrow. But the Lord is always with us; and He grants unto us peace, strength, and fruitfulness. May our prayer be: "Let the beauty of the Lord our God be upon us: and establish Thou the work of our hands."*

V. TOWARDS EVENING.

The transition from one age of life to another is never abrupt. It comes gradually and almost imperceptibly. We know that it has come, but not when it set in. There is a point in mature manhood when there is a transition, the beginning

* Ps. xc. 17.

of the descent. The simplest indication of it is when the thought awakes vividly within us—we have finished more than the half of our journey, we shall not be as long in the world as we have been already. In childhood, in youth, in early manhood, life lies before us like a large unbounded plain, or like a high mountain; but when we come to the summit a new prospect opens before us, a downward path leading to the ocean of death and eternity. Then we understand what the disciples felt on their way to Emmaus, when they said: "It is toward evening, and the day is far spent."

A greater seriousness and stillness takes hold of our spirits. We are more inclined to commune with ourselves. We are more anxious to be, than to seem. Many have been our disappointments, chiefly with ourselves. We begin to ask ourselves how we have kept "that which was committed to us."* We feel that we have possessed less strength than we thought, less devotedness, loyalty, perseverance. Many flowers of promise have vanished and brought forth no fruit. Many tasks have been left unaccomplished, many opportunities remained neglected or misused. Much that cannot be remedied passes before our mind and weighs down our hearts. We are tempted to be weary, and to

* 1 Tim. vi. 20.

yield to despondency. Let us rouse ourselves, and hear the call to be steadfast, and to persevere to the end. This our sad experience may become a source of blessing. When we are chastened and truly humbled, when we have found how weak we are and how little we have done, God may prolong our days, and use us more than ever as instruments of His grace and power. Jesus said: "As long as I am in the world, I am the light of the world." The day-labourer has no right to conclude his work until the master summons him. God will also supply all needful grace and strength. The Lord may be keeping the best wine to the last; and it may be true of us also:

> "Ever the richest, tenderest glow
> Sets round the autumnal sun."

VI. OLD AGE.

Lastly comes old age. It ought to be the most beautiful season of our life, combining all the valuable elements of our past.

Old age is venerable. God Himself is called the Ancient of Days, and He commanded the children of Israel to show reverence to the old, to rise before the hoary head, and to honour the face of the old man.* Now the character is matured.

* Lev. xix. 32.

The results of our experience, of our thought and information, have been winnowed, and have formed themselves into a condensed treasury of terse and lucid wisdom. Old age is venerable, because it reminds us of eternity. Childhood and youth, and even manhood, remind us of the rapid flight of Time. In them we look forward to the quiet years of our old age. But when old age has actually come, we look forward to eternity. Soon will the aged man be ushered into the eternal world, and be initiated into its mysteries. In youth and manhood there is also constant change and activity. The quiet and calmness of old age brings before us the everlasting, unchanging Present.

Scripture does not conceal the infirmities and troubles of old age. Its gloomy aspects are brought before us with graphic power in the last chapter of Ecclesiastes. Scripture does not deny that in one view we say of our last years, "I have no pleasure in them." But how full and glorious is Scripture's description of the perennial youth, peace, strength, and joy of God's children! In the very psalm which describes man as a frail flower of the field, David praises the Lord, who renews our youth as the eagle. God is the God of the aged. Even to old age, to hoar hairs, will

I carry you; I will bear; I will deliver you.* The righteous shall flourish as the palm tree, and bring forth fruit in old age. The apostle Paul confesses that our old man perishes visibly and daily; but he adds, the inner man is renewed day by day.† So then for the inner man there is no old age, no decay, no downward descent. He possesses youthful vitality. Only children and young people grow day by day. Thus is it with the Christian. In old age his inner man grows in peace, in light, in strength. The outer world becomes dim; but the spiritual and eternal world more distinct. Knowledge grows fuller; he comprehends the length and breadth, and height and depth; he beholds more clearly the city which hath foundations. His meditations discover wonder upon wonder. Endless are the objects of interest. Fathers know Him who is from the beginning. Christ, who has been their teacher for years, recapitulates as it were all the glorious lessons of the past with greater simplicity and comprehensiveness. Christ Himself is seen in greater fulness and glory. As knowledge expands, adoration also becomes more profound.

The life of the affections also is in youthful vigour. Now the self-asserting will is more quiet;

---

* Isa. xlvi. 4. † 2 Cor. iv. 16.

we think no longer of our name, of our task, of our portion of the Church, but the grand old petitions of our dear "Our Father"—Thy name be hallowed. Thy kingdom come. Thy will be done in earth, as it is in heaven—ascend from our souls with childlike simplicity. We love all Christians; we rejoice in every progress of God's work; we give thanks for those that have departed in peace, and we look forward with glowing hearts to the time when the glory of the Lord shall fill the whole earth. Who has not seen old Christians, such as I describe, loving children of God, loyal disciples of Christ, full of affection to Christ's people, and of goodwill towards all men?

It is the charm of youth that it is the age of hope. The world lies before it. But even in this, old age has the brightness of youth; for the lively hope of our eternal inheritance is then felt as never before. May it not be the special task of old age to enter more fully into the spirit of hope, one of the three fundamental graces, which perhaps is practically not considered as frequently and earnestly as faith and love? "Rejoicing in hope" is the attitude of the aged Christian. We remember the beautiful description which Bunyan gives in his *Pilgrim's Progress* of the land of Beulah. How transparent and true to faith is the language of symbolic imagery. "The air of this country is very sweet and pleasant. Every day the flowers appear in the earth, and the voice of the turtle is heard in the land. Here they were within sight of the city they were going to; also here met them some of the inhabitants thereof; for in this land the shining ones commonly walked, because it was upon the borders of heaven. In this land also the contract between the Bridegroom and Bride was renewed. Here they heard voices from the city, loud voices, saying, 'Say ye to the daughter of Zion, Behold, thy salvation cometh; behold, His reward is with Him.'"

God has assigned unto old age a special testimony. Only the aged can confirm their testimony by the impressive preface, "I have been young, and now am old." The words of Paul the aged come with great power and with touching pathos. John, the beloved disciple, writes in his old age. The wisdom, simplicity, and tenderness of his teaching are the result of long years of communion with God. We feel as if the venerable apostle was still carried into the assembly of the saints, and as if we heard his voice—"Children, love one another."

Is it not delightful to think of the aged servants of God who were permitted to work and witness for many years?—of Moses, who was an hundred and twenty years old when he died (his eye was not dim, nor his natural force abated); of Caleb, who followed the Lord fully, and was strong and vigorous when he had reached the age of eighty-five years; of Samuel, whose prophetic life commenced in his childhood and continued with steadfast brightness and loyalty to the last; of Jehoiada, who did good toward the Lord and toward the house of God till he was one hundred and thirty years old, and then was buried in the city of David among the kings of Israel; of Hosea, who exercised for more than seventy years the office of a prophet among God's people? We see the bright and venerable countenances of Simeon, chief singer of the choir of veterans, and of Hannah, who, a hundred and three years old, was like a youthful evangelist announcing the advent of Messiah to the faithful in Jerusalem. "Eighty and six years have I served Jesus, my Lord," was the confession of Polycarp, who then went through a martyr's death to his Saviour's bosom.*

Martin Luther, speaking on one occasion about our earthly life and the history of mankind, said that "Time was like a very long beam, and that

---

* Deuteronomy xxxiv. 7; Joshua xiv. 10; 2 Chronicles xxiv. 15, 16.

we time-bound beings look at it lengthwise, and it appears to us very long and protracted; but God looks at it breadthwise, and it appears to Him but a moment." We also shall at last reach the mountain-height from which the whole ascending path with its many windings shall be seen. "It doth not yet appear what we shall be," said even the highly-favoured Seer of the new covenant; and we must all confess with that eminent servant of God who meditated much on the Saints' Everlasting Rest: "My knowledge of that life is small." But the Scripture reveals to us sufficiently the nature of our future blessedness, to enable us to form a true estimate of earthly life, and to experience the purifying as well as consoling character of Christian hope.

We behold the widest diversity in the great multitude which no man can number. Both young men and maidens, old men and children, gathered from among all nations and kindreds, praise the Lord and serve Him day and night in His heavenly sanctuary. But much more striking than their diversity is their oneness; they form one family, and present the same glorious appearance. In a world where all is bright and pure, among the holy and perfect angels, the cherubim and seraphim, the redeemed from among men shine forth with a transcendant whiteness. "What are these which are arrayed in white robes?" How bright these glorious spirits shine! They are not angels, but the sinners of Adam's race saved by the Son of God. They are Christ's. They "have washed their robes, and made them white in the blood of the Lamb." They stand now before God and the Lamb because the blood of Jesus Christ, the Son of God, cleansed them from all sin, and redeemed them to be a kingdom of priests. By Christ they entered, and in Christ they stand. And as Christ is their righteousness, so He is also their life. Christ is not merely upon them, but in them. They resemble the Lord Jesus in His love. They bear the image of the heavenly, the second Adam. They are pure and spotless, the sons of God. Their very bodies are like Christ's glorious body. Their earthly sufferings and trials only identify them with their Saviour. Jesus, who became in all things like unto them, sin excepted, that He might suffer and die in their stead, has now made them in all things like unto Himself, except His incommunicable divinity. He is their Lord, their Head, their adorable Shepherd; He is the Lamb that is worthy of divine honour, and they are the Lamb's wife. Christ is all—their righteousness, their life, their joy; from Him, in Him, and with Him they receive all things to the glory of the Father.

This, then, ought to be our life-long aim and desire, to win Christ, that we may be found in Him, having the righteousness which is of God, and that we may live the life of faith and bring forth the fruits of the Spirit.

Justification and sanctification are given unto us the moment we believe in Jesus, because Christ is then ours. We are then accepted in Christ; we are also renewed by the Spirit of God and grafted into the living Vine. But all our subsequent life we are occupied with justification and sanctification; with the former pre-eminently; for it is the source and strength of our spiritual life. We must learn daily what is implied by coming to God through Jesus, in His name, by faith in His blood. We are often brought into the lowest hell, and emptied of all our believing and rejoicing, to learn again that salvation is by grace. It is by our daily repentance towards God and faith in the Lord Jesus that we *live*, that we resist and overcome sin, that we walk in the footsteps of our Master.

Let us then cling to our Lord Jesus Christ. We live on what He is and what He has for us. And let us measure all earthly trials, sorrows, joys, possessions, attainments, by their relation to our true life, blessedness and riches. One thing let us desire and seek after, that through eternity we may be before God in Christ and like Christ; that at present we may learn of Jesus, who is meek and lowly in heart; that we may be rich in heavenly treasure, in the knowledge of God, in faith, in patience, in humility, in love; and that we may be faithful stewards and servants, loyal to our divine Head. And while it is day let us work the works of Christ who sent us. While there are still poor and needy, lonely and sorrowful, tempted and struggling ones; while there is still the going forth of the good Shepherd, seeking to save the lost and to restore the wayward, let us be Christ's representatives, messengers, channels. Let us not be weary in well-doing; let us always abound in the work of the Lord, forasmuch as we know that our labour is not in vain in the Lord.*

"While it is day!" The night cometh when no man can work. The night cometh when none can enter in at the strait gate; when the message is no longer sent to us: "This is the work of God, that ye believe in Him whom He hath sent." Is this not a solemn thought to those who are still without Christ? It is not the preacher, it is not a peculiar school of theology, it is *God Himself*

---

* 1 Cor. xv. 58 (notice connection).

who limiteth the day, and saith: "To-day if ye will hear His voice harden not your hearts." When the night cometh it brings deliverance from all evil to the Christian; but what does it bring to the Christless man? Does death free him from the love and power of sin? or from its guilt and condemnation? It is not death, but Christ, who is the Saviour; it is not by dying, but by believing in Jesus, that we are pardoned and renewed. Does death deliver him from misery and pain? Death only reveals the true condition of the soul; and the rich man, we read, lifted up his eyes in Hades, being in torments. The only thing from which death separates the Christless man for ever is the influence of divine grace. The Father will no longer say to him, "Return unto Me." The voice of the gentle Shepherd will no more go forth, "Come unto Me." The Holy Ghost will no longer witness of God's salvation. Sin remains; sorrow remains; God is lost. Look at the Christian. When he dies he is delivered from sin. Christ had already delivered him from the guilt and the dominion of sin; now he is delivered also from its presence. Without spot, or blemish, or wrinkle, free from all sin and conflict, the child of God is presented unblameable before God's throne. When the Christian dies he is delivered from all pain and suffering. He is carried by the angels into the bosom of perfect love and peace. In the land whither he goes there is no more sorrow nor crying; "they shall hunger no more, nor thirst any more; neither shall the sun light on them, nor any heat." But Jesus will be theirs. They shall see Him as He is. They shall know, even as they are known. They shall say, as they were never able to say on earth, "God is my sure portion, and my exceeding great reward."

"There shall be no night there; and they need no candle, neither light of the sun; for the glory of the Lord doth lighten the city, and the Lamb is the light thereof."

Let us not neglect so great salvation while it is day. WHILE IT IS DAY!

www.ingramcontent.com/pod-product-compliance
Lightning Source LLC
Chambersburg PA
CBHW022113160426
43197CB00009B/1007